AL-GHAZĀLĪ

The Institute of Ismaili Studies
Ismaili Heritage Series, 5
General Editor: Farhad Daftary

Previously published titles:

1. Paul E. Walker, *Abū Yaʿqūb al-Sijistānī: Intellectual Missionary* (1996)
2. Heinz Halm, *The Fatimids and their Traditions of Learning* (1997)
3. Paul E. Walker, *Ḥamīd al-Dīn al-Kirmānī: Ismaili Thought in the Age of al-Ḥākim* (1999)
4. Alice C. Hunsberger, *Nasir Khusraw, The Ruby of Badakhshan: A Portrait of the Persian Poet, Traveller and Philosopher* (2000)

Al-Ghazālī and the Ismailis

A Debate on Reason and Authority in Medieval Islam

FAROUK MITHA

I.B.Tauris *Publishers*
LONDON • NEW YORK
in association with
The Institute of Ismaili Studies
LONDON

Published in 2001 by I.B.Tauris & Co Ltd
6 Salem Rd, London W2 4BU
175 Fifth Avenue, New York NY 10010
www.ibtauris.com

in association with The Institute of Ismaili Studies
42–44 Grosvenor Gardens, London SW1W OEB
www.iis.ac.uk

In the United States of America and in Canada distributed by
St Martin's Press, 175 Fifth Avenue, New York NY 10010

ISBN 186064 792 8

A full CIP record for this book is available from the British Library
A full CIP record for this book is available from the Library of Congress

Library of Congress catalog card: available

Typeset in ITC New Baskerville by Hepton Books, Oxford
Printed and bound in Great Britain by MPG Books Ltd, Bodmin, Cornwall

The Institute of Ismaili Studies

The Institute of Ismaili Studies was established in 1977 with the object of promoting scholarship and learning on Islam, in the historical as well as contemporary contexts, and a better understanding of its relationship with other societies and faiths.

The Institute's programmes encourage a perspective which is not confined to the theological and religious heritage of Islam, but seek to explore the relationship of religious ideas to broader dimensions of society and culture. The programmes thus encourage an interdisciplinary approach to the materials of Islamic history and thought. Particular attention is also given to issues of modernity that arise as Muslims seek to relate their heritage to the contemporary situation.

Within the Islamic tradition, the Institute's programmes seek to promote research on those areas which have, to date, received relatively little attention from scholars. These include the intellectual and literary expressions of Shiʿism in general, and Ismailism in particular.

In the context of Islamic societies, the Institute's programmes are informed by the full range and diversity of cultures in which Islam is practised today, from the Middle East, South and Central

Asia and Africa to the industrialized societies of the West, thus taking into consideration the variety of contexts which shape the ideals, beliefs and practices of the faith.

These objectives are realized through concrete programmes and activities organised and implemented by various departments of the Institute. The Institute also collaborates periodically, on a programme-specific basis, with other institutions of learning in the United Kingdom and abroad.

The Institute's academic publications fall into several distinct and interrelated categories:

1. Occasional papers or essays addressing broad themes of the relationship between religion and society, with special reference to Islam.
2. Monographs exploring specific aspects of Islamic faith and culture, or the contributions of individual Muslim figures or writers.
3. Editions or translations of significant primary or secondary texts.
4. Translations of poetic or literary texts which illustrate the rich heritage of spiritual, devotional and symbolic expressions in Muslim history.
5. Works on Ismaili history and thought, and the relationship of the Ismailis to other traditions, communities and schools of thought in Islam.
6. Proceedings of conferences and seminars sponsored by the Institute.
7. Bibliographical works and catalogues which document manuscripts, printed texts and other source materials.

This book falls into category five listed above.

In facilitating these and other publications, the Institute's sole aim is to encourage original research and analysis of relevant issues. While every effort is made to ensure that the publications are of a high academic standard, there is naturally bound to be a diversity of views, ideas and interpretations. As such, the opinions expressed in these publications are to be understood as belonging to their authors alone.

Ismaili Heritage Series

A major Shiʿi Muslim community, the Ismailis have had a long and eventful history. Scattered in many regions of the world, in Asia, Africa, Europe and North America, the Ismailis have elaborated diverse intellectual and literary traditions in different languages. On two occasions they had states of their own, the Fatimid caliphate and the Nizari state of Iran and Syria during the Alamut period. While pursuing particular religio-political aims, the leaders of these Ismaili states also variously encouraged intellectual, scientific, artistic and commercial activities.

Until recently, the Ismailis were studied and judged almost exclusively on the basis of the evidence collected or fabricated by their enemies, including the bulk of the medieval heresiographers and polemicists who were hostile towards the Shiʿa in general and the Ismailis among them in particular. These authors in fact treated the Shiʿi interpretations of Islam as expressions of heterodoxy or even heresy. As a result, a 'black legend' was gradually developed and put into circulation in the Muslim world to discredit the Ismailis and their interpretation of Islam. The Christian Crusaders and their occidental chroniclers, who remained almost completely ignorant of Islam and its internal divisions, disseminated their own myths of the Ismailis, which came to be accepted in Europe as true descriptions of Ismaili teachings and practices. Modern orientalists, too, have studied the Ismailis on the basis of these hostile sources and fanciful accounts of medieval times. Thus, legends and misconceptions have continued to surround the Ismailis through the twentieth century.

In more recent decades, however, the field of Ismaili studies has been revolutionized due to the recovery and study of genuine Ismaili sources on a large scale – manuscript materials which in different ways survived the destruction of the Fatimid and Nizari Ismaili libraries. These sources, representing diverse literary traditions produced in Arabic, Persian and Indic languages, had hitherto been secretly preserved in private collections in India, Central Asia, Iran, Afghanistan, Syria and the Yemen.

Modern progress in Ismaili studies has already necessitated a complete re-writing of the history of the Ismailis and their contributions to Islamic civilization. It has now become clear that the Ismailis founded important libraries and institutions of learning such as al-Azhar and the Dar al-ʿIlm in Cairo, while some of their learned *daʿis* or missionaries developed unique intellectual traditions amalgamating their theological doctrine with a diversity of philosophical traditions in complex metaphysical systems. The Ismaili patronage of learning and extension of hospitality to non-Ismaili scholars was maintained even in such difficult times as the Alamut period, when the community was preoccupied with its survival in an extremely hostile milieu.

The Ismaili Heritage Series, published under the auspices of the Department of Academic Research and Publications of The Institute of Ismaili Studies, aims to make available to wide audiences the results of modern scholarship on the Ismailis and their rich intellectual and cultural heritage, as well as certain aspects of their more recent history and achievements.

For Munni,
who makes everything so complete

Contents

Foreword

Al-Ghazālī's writings in a variety of Islamic disciplines display not only remarkable intellectual tenacity and curiosity but also a near-obsessive quest for epistemic certainty which eventually led this illustrious thinker to embrace Sufism. For these and other reasons, he has received a greater share of attention from modern scholars than any other medieval Muslim figure. The production of yet another book on al-Ghazālī might seem redundant, but this is certainly not the case with the book presented here. The reader is offered a perceptive reading of al-Ghazālī's *Kitāb al-Mustaẓhirī* in which the author engages in a critical dialogue with Ismaili doctrines during the Fatimid and early Alamūt periods. Having provided an account of the religious and political background of the treatise in question, Farouk Mitha sheds significant light on al-Ghazālī's relationship with the Ismailis and the manner he was influenced by their thought. This last theme further enhances the provocative bent of this study.

The strength of the present work lies in its close textual analysis, as well as in the way in which it situates al-Ghazālī's text within a wider intellectual and political history of ideas. The *Kitāb al-Mustaẓhirī* serves as an instructive example for the study and understanding of central questions in medieval Islamic thought, and Mitha's work does due justice to the intellectual complexity and significance of these questions. The work is particularly commendable for bringing into sharper focus questions related to the manner in which the concept of authority was problematized in medieval Islam, encompassing, as it were, the dividing lines between Sunni and Shiʿi thought; between scriptural-based and rational modes of thought and reasoning; and between the evolving conceptions of spiritual (*dīn*) and temporal (*dunyā*) authority. Al-Ghazālī's discourse is perceived here as engaged in and engaging a political and religious reality, and not merely as theological abstraction. Such an interpretive approach makes any reading that separates the text from its environment obsolete.

This book no doubt fills some hitherto unnoticed gaps, and in the process offers us stimulating insights into al-Ghazālī's thought and on the influential role of Ismaili doctrines in Muslim intellectual history.

Wael B. Hallaq
McGill University

Preface

Ideas have a history, and their history is rarely simple. Great ideas are those that have changed the world, the most enduring of which develop and express themselves as a new vision for humanity. The phenomenon of scriptural religion provides us with a rich historical example of the power of visionary ideas – ideas that, over time, become ideals as it were for the development of an entire culture, and in some cases even a civilization. Islam is one such phenomenon, a set of ideas beginning with an experience of prophetic revelation, yet ever widening into a scripture, a community, a tradition, an empire and a civilization. At the heart of the Islamic phenomenon is a vision and an ethos; its history, stretching as it does over a millennium and a half, and continuing, embraces almost every conceivable dimension of human life.

The study of any one aspect of Islamic history, be it in the area of thought, culture or society, should not be disengaged from the idea of Islam as an embodiment of an encompassing vision and ethos. In the words of Marshall G.S. Hodgson, Islam is a 'venture' embodying both a 'conscience' and a 'history'.[1]

This study is about one text and its author, and their relationship to a specific moment in the history of Islam. *Faḍā'iḥ al-Bāṭiniyya wa faḍā'il al-Mustaẓhiriyya* (The Infamies of the Bāṭiniyya and the Virtues of the Mustaẓhiriyya) – more commonly referred to as the *Kitāb al-Mustaẓhirī* – is the title of the text, and Muḥammad Abū Ḥāmid al-Ghazālī (d.505/1111), the author. Al-Ghazālī is arguably one of the most influential thinkers in the history of Islamic thought, and one whose writings have received greater attention from Western scholars than those of any other Muslim thinker. The aim of this study is to understand the ideas and arguments of his *Kitāb al-Mustaẓhirī* and the disposition of the author when writing it. More importantly, it sets out to understand the broader historical configuration of ideas and tensions in which, it will be argued, the text was situated, and with which it was inextricably engaged. In effect, this study seeks to re-evaluate the historical significance of *K. al-Mustaẓhirī*, and put forward new explanations, building on those of other scholars, of al-Ghazālī's motives for writing it.

With the emergence of the written word, texts have become the quintessential repositories of ideas; hence, a history of ideas is, broadly speaking, tantamount to a history of texts. This study, in pursuing the aims outlined above, will treat *K. al-Mustaẓhirī*, as a repository, and will explore the key ideas of which it is a repository, thereby opening broader questions of how and in what senses the text is emblematic of the nature and fabric of medieval Muslim society and thought. It should, however, be borne in mind that this is no more than a preliminary exploration. A more exhaustive historical analysis, drawing on a much broader range of sources, and demanding, as it would, an examination of the *K. al-Mustaẓhirī* against the background of al-Ghazālī's entire body of writing has yet to be undertaken. The intention here is to propose new, relatively unexplored, ways of reading *K. al-Mustaẓhirī*, and thus, by extension, to raise new questions about our understanding of al-Ghazālī and of the age in which he lived.

FM
Victoria B.C

Acknowledgements

Had it not been for those nagging questions that kept puzzling me every time I tried to trace the connections between al-Ghazālī and the Ismailis, this book may not have been written. I am thus simply grateful for the persistence with which those questions kept visiting me, and only hope that I have done them due justice in this book.

The writing of this book entailed a long and rewarding journey into the intellectual world of medieval Islamic thought, a world which, rather like a kaleidoscope, continues to offer up new patterns and associations to my modern, quizzical eye. During the process of writing this book and in preparing it for publication, I have become indebted to many individuals. To Professor Wael Hallaq, I owe several debts. It was he who first suggested the idea for this study while I was a graduate student at McGill University, and having planted the idea, guided me patiently as I tried to find my way inside the texts and arguments of medieval Islamic law and theology. His prolific and path-breaking writings on Islamic law and Muslim intellectual history have served as my touchstones. I want to also thank him for writing the Foreword.

I am extremely grateful to Dr Farhad Daftary for all his support and for recommending this study for publication by The Institute of Ismaili Studies. From Dr Aziz Esmail I have received invaluable intellectual stimulation over the years; our conversations together always leave me feeling more curious and alert. Many thanks to Patricia Salazar for editorial advice and assistance.

To Alnoor Merchant, fellow comrade, I want to express my special gratitude for making books available to me from the Institute's library and his own private collection, and for identifying the manuscript page used in the jacket design of this publication.

For the delight and enthusiasm shared in seeing the book come to light, I want to thank all the immediate members of the Mitha and Gova family in Vancouver and Toronto, the Moosa family in Toronto, Lisa Herising and Roshni Narain in Victoria, and Mohamed Alibhai in Olympia.

Regardless of the nagging questions that got me started, the completion of this work would not have been possible without the continuing generosity and inspiration from my wife, Mehmoona.

Chronology

al-Ghazālī	Saljuqs and Caliph al-Mustaẓhir	Ismailis
		358/969: The Fatimids enter Egypt and establish the city of Cairo, which becomes the capital of the Fatimid Ismaili state.
	447/1055: Ṭughril Beg marches into Baghdad and establishes Saljuq rule under the symbolic authority of the Abbasid caliph al-Qā'im.	**427–487/1036–1094**: Al-Mustanṣir reigns from Cairo as the Fatimid Caliph-Imam for almost 60 years.
450/1058: Born at Ṭūs in northern Iran.	**455–485/1072–1092**: Niẓām al-Mulk appointed *wazīr*. Consolidates Saljuq power in Iraq and Iran under Alp Arslān and Malik Shāh. In 459/1067 establishes the Niẓāmiyya college in Baghdad.	
c. 470–478/1077–1085: Studies under al-Juwaynī (d.478/1085).		**471–473/1078–1081**: Ḥasan-i Ṣabbāḥ trains as an Ismaili *dā'ī* in Fatimid Egypt.
478–484/1085–1091: Attached to Niẓām al-Mulk's camp-court.		**483/1090**: Ḥasan-i Ṣabbāḥ takes over the mountain fortress of Alamūt in northern Iran which was later to become the headquarters of the Nizārī Ismaili state and *da'wa*.
484–488/1091–1095: Teaches Shāfi'ī law at the Niẓāmiyya college	**485/1092**: Malik Shāh dies. A civil war over the succession breaks	

in Baghdad. Key texts written in this period include: *Maqāṣid al-falāsifa; Tahāfut al-falāsifa; Kitāb al-Mustaẓhirī; al-Iqtiṣād-fi’l-iʿtiqād.*	out within the Saljuq clan. Niẓām al-Mulk is assassinated.	The state was organized around a network of mountain fortresses in Iran and Syria.
488–499/1095–1106: After undergoing a personal crisis, al-Ghazālī departs suddenly from Baghdad. Becomes a reclusive traveller and embraces Sufi ideals, spending extended periods in Damascus, Jerusalem, Mecca and Medina. Composes his major work *Iḥyā ʿulūm al-dīn.*	**487/1094**: The young al-Mustaẓhir becomes Abbasid caliph in the midst of the Saljuq civil war.	**487/1094**: After the death of the Caliph-Imam al-Mustanṣir, a succession dispute between his sons Nizār and al-Mustaʿlī, splits the Ismaili community and *daʿwa* into Nizārī and Mustaʿlī factions.
499–503/1106–1109: Returns to Nīshāpūr where he takes up a teaching position at the *madrasa*. Writes his intellectual autobiography *al-Munqidh min al-ḍalāl.*	**488/1095** onwards: As a result of the civil war the Saljuq sultanate is divided into eastern and western territories. Berkiyāruq (d.498/1105) consolidates power in the east and Tutush (d.488/1095) in the west.	**488/1095**: Ḥasan-i Ṣabbāḥ champions the cause of Nizar. The doctrine of *taʿlim* becomes prominent in the consolidation of Nizārī Ismailism.
505/1111: Dies at Ṭūs.		**518/1124**: Ḥasan-i Ṣabbāḥ dies at Alamūt.
	590/1194: Saljuq rule in Iraq and Iran comes to an end.	**654/1256**: The Mongols capture Alamūt and within two years sack Baghdad, uprooting the Abbasid caliphate.

Tradition is a matter of much wider significance. It cannot be inherited, and if you want it you must obtain it by great labour. It involves, in the first place, the historical sense ... This historical sense, which is a sense of the timeless as well as of the temporal and of the timeless and of the temporal together, is what makes a writer traditional. And it is at the same time what makes a writer most acutely conscious of his place in time, of his own contemporaneity.

T.S. Eliot

CHAPTER ONE

Ecology of the *Kitāb al-Mustaẓhirī*: Historical Place and Time

There is an extensive and distinguished body of scholarship in European languages on al-Ghazālī. Apart from the numerous monographs and articles on his life and thought, including the large number of critical editions and translations of his texts, there is one topic of particular significance which stands out, and which has attracted the efforts of some of the leading scholars in Islamic Studies. Beginning with Ignaz Goldziher and continuing with Louis Massignon, Asín Palacios, W.M. Watt, M. Bouyges, A. Badawi and G.F. Hourani, all have attempted to construct a chronology of al-Ghazālī's writings.[1] These attempts at a chronology are indicative of an attitude prevalent in the study of al-Ghazālī, namely, that his writings are intimately connected with, and hence cannot be seen apart from, the circumstances of his life.

Al-Ghazālī, in his autobiography entitled *al-Munqidh min al-ḍalāl* (Deliverance from Error), constructs a schematic picture of his life (450–505/1058–1111), ordered around his different attitudes to knowledge and the nature of truth.[2] These attitudes are seen as representing intellectual stages, each of which, he claims, spurred him to write, and hence in the *Munqidh* he classifies some of his major writings within the framework of these stages. Much has been written about the authenticity, value and uniqueness of *al-Munqidh min al-ḍalāl*, and it has had a powerful influence in shaping the image of al-Ghazālī in orientalist scholarship as a remarkably self-aware, pre-modern religious thinker, propelled by an existential yet disciplined curiosity embracing *fiqh* (law), *kalām* (theology), *falsafa* (philosophy) and *taṣawwuf* (Sufism or mysticism).[3] It tells of a life not lacking in dramatic tension, at the centre of which is his much discussed personal crisis and sudden departure from Baghdad in Dhu'l-Qa'da 488/November 1095, after which he turned into a reclusive traveller, returning almost eleven years later to a life dedicated to Sufi ideals.[4]

The importance of a chronology becomes increasingly clear, enabling us not only to graft a sense of order on to al-Ghazālī's prolific output of writings, estimated at some forty titles, but, and more importantly, to discern a line of development in his thought that so clearly was subject to several significant turning points throughout his life. His texts bear witness to these turning points, each with its own distinctive face, capturing, in turn, not only the unusual texture of his life but also the range of his many different voices – each worthy of study. This intellectual range and vitality explains, in part, the fascination of orientalist scholarship with his life and writings. However, despite the diverse themes and styles of writing, al-Ghazālī's extant texts constitute an integrated fabric, replete with cross-references to each other, and imbued with a passionate and consistent concern for the community of Muslims for whom he was writing.

It is with these considerations that we will now approach the *K. al-Mustaẓhirī*, asking questions related to its dating and position in the fabric of al-Ghazālī's writings, to the nature of the turning points in al-Ghazālī's life that may have shaped the writing of this text, and to the types of communal concerns to which al-Ghazālī was then responding.

As for dating the *K. al-Mustaẓhirī*, there is general scholarly agreement that it was composed prior to his departure from Baghdad in Dhu'l-Qa'da 488/November 1095, and definitely no earlier than 15 Muḥarram, 487/4 February, 1094. The latter date refers to al-Mustaẓhir's accession to office as caliph and as such becomes a benchmark, since the text is formally addressed to al-Mustaẓhir (d.512/1118) who, al-Ghazālī claims, commissioned him to write it. With reference to the relative chronological position of the *K. al-Mustaẓhirī*, the most rigorously constructed inter-textual analysis is that of George F. Hourani, who, in relation to al-Ghazālī's better known texts, places it before *al-Iqtiṣād fi'l-iʿtiqād* (Moderation in Belief) and after *Tahāfut al-falāsifa* (The Incoherence of the Philosophers).[5]

Before examining the nature of the turning points that may have influenced the writing of this text, a few general comments will be made as to what exactly is implied by this term. The study of history begins inevitably with retrospection, leading to an awareness of the distance, ever increasing, between the moment of retrospection and the ever-growing landscape of the past. Entering into any one area of this landscape is essentially a mental act. An act, which besides relying on memory, written records and all manner of identifiable traces, is nevertheless shaped by our images of the past. Turning points are one such image. This is most clearly evident in our periodization of history. We find, for example, the personification of time in relation to an ideal of Classicism, hence the emergence of various classical periods, and the subsequent progressive or declining march of time; or the description of forms of revolutionary change which have a long-term impact on the life of human cultures and societies, designated by terms ranging, for example, from the Axial Age, the Renaissance to the Enlightenment.

The study of Islamic history is no exception; its stock of turning-point images has its source in both Muslim historiography and in orientalist scholarship. The turning points to be examined in this study are of a far smaller scale and limited to the landscape of fifth/eleventh-century Baghdad. The *K. al-Mustaẓhirī* will serve as our place of entry into this landscape, and the Saljuqs, the Sunni Abbasid caliphate and the Ismailis – each with their own distinctive set of images – will serve as points of focus from which the nature of the turning points in this landscape will be analysed. Of the three parties, the *K. al-Mustaẓhirī* addresses directly the Sunni caliph and the Ismailis (variously referred to as al-Bāṭiniyya or al-Taʿlīmiyya), while the Saljuqs are referred to only indirectly. The significance of each party will be viewed in light of al-Ghazālī's historical relationship to them, leading thereafter to an examination of the manner in which each was represented and interpreted in the *K. al-Mustaẓhirī*. In effect, the *K. al-Mustaẓhirī* embodies a dialogue with each one of these parties, and it is by analysis of the concepts and images associated with each of these dialogues that we will endeavour to re-read its historical significance.

Al-Ghazālī and the Saljuqs

The 'Age of the Saljuqs' is emblematic of several important turning points in Islamic history, and particularly that of Iran and Iraq – the so-called central Islamic lands. There is a significant body of scholarship on Saljuq history, touching on the social, political, religious and intellectual dimensions of the period, and covered with a remarkable degree of depth and sophistication compared with research in other similar areas or periods of medieval history. The most significant research is contained in the writings of Claude Cahen – whose several monographs and many articles have clearly set the foundation on which all subsequent scholarship on the Saljuqs has developed[6] – as well as those of Ann K.S. Lambton and George Makdisi.

The interpretations of Saljuq history have been formulated around the following three themes: (i) the nature of the Turkic migrations and their concomitant consolidation of power; (ii) the elaboration of a distinctive political and economic structure in an ever-expanding Saljuq empire; and (iii) the ideological and intellectual revival of Sunni Islam. Lambton's writings, building on those of Cahen, have focused on the second theme, while Makdisi, in many ways breaking new ground, has focused on the third.[7]

Before bringing al-Ghazālī into the picture, let us briefly review some of the presuppositions and conclusions in these themes. As regards the Turkic background of the Saljuqs, this can be best approached by beginning with the establishment of Buwayhid control over Baghdad in 334/945. The rise of the Buwayhids, a family of Daylamī soldiers, marked the most decisive and well organized infiltration into the central Islamic lands by one of the many emerging non-Arab tribes, whose earliest traces date to the beginning of the third/ninth century. Their geographical origins can be traced back to the amorphous tribal groupings around the edges of the northeastern borders of the Islamic world, the Gurgān-Dihistān region to the southeast of the Caspian Sea, Khwārazm, Transoxania and probably also eastern Afghanistan.[8] The influence of Turkic tribal interests grew significantly with the introduction of Turkish slaves into the then dissipating caliphal armies, and subsequent recruitment of Turkish mercenaries during the reign of Caliph al-Muʿtaṣim (*r.*232–247/847–861). By the middle of the fourth/tenth century the Turkish element had burgeoned into a major power bloc which directly threatened the authority of the Abbasid caliph.[9]

Manifestations of this threat began with the murder of Caliph al-Mutawakkil in 248/862, followed by the gradual fragmentation of the Abbasid empire and the consequent marginalization of the power and role of the caliphate. It was upon this state of affairs that the Buwayhids established their confederation, encompassing Iraq and western Iran with branches of the family based in Baghdad. Muʿizz al-Dawla (d.356/967), a Buwayhid chief, proclaimed himself *amīr al-umarāʾ* and thereby ingeniously maintained, albeit symbolically, the authority of the caliphal court while legitimizing himself as the commander-in-chief – the *de facto* holder of power. The maintenance of Buwayhid power (lasting for more than a century) was due not only to the regime of brute force, but also to the revival of the evocative mould of pre-Islamic Sassanid kingship within which they portrayed themselves as more than just the chiefs of nomadic soldiers.[10] This historical split between power and authority was henceforth to become the enduring tension in all subsequent conceptions and embodiments of government in Muslim societies. In the case of the Buwayhids, this tension was further accentuated by the fact that they identified themselves as Imami (or Twelver) Shiʿa, while simultaneously projecting themselves as protectors of the Sunni caliph. Indeed their Shiʿi sympathies were of no token character.

With their arrival, following shortly after the advent of the *ghayba al-kubrā* (greater occultation) of the twelfth Imam in 329/941, Baghdad became a prominent centre of Imami Shiʿi learning and scholarship.

The Buwayhid period set in motion a number of far-reaching transformations. First, the definitions of political authority were reformulated through the inauguration of a distinct juridico-political (*siyāsa sharʿiyya*) tradition of writing – the first major exponent being al-Māwardī (d.450/1058). Second, the structures of territorial governance and land use in the central Islamic lands were transformed through the implementation of the *iqṭāʿ* (denoting an assignment or a grant of land as a source of revenue). Third, the ethnic make-up in this area became more diverse, and the Turkish element was to play a dominant role. Finally, the demarcations and differences distinguishing Shiʿism from Sunnism became more self-conscious, and were debated with a greater polemical intensity. All these developments were to be further accelerated and given new life with the coming of the Saljuqs.

The background of the Saljuqs can be traced to the Oghuz tribes east of the Aral Sea. Their grand entrance into the annals of Islamic history began with Ṭughril Beg (d. 455/1063), one of the chiefs of the Saljuq clan, who marched into Baghdad in 447/1055 and, as the sources inform us, liberated the caliph from the clutches of the Shiʿi Buwayhids. Thereafter he proclaimed himself sultan in place of the Buwayhid *amīr*.[11] By this time, all the territories formerly ruled by the Buwayhids had passed into the hands of the Saljuqs, and by the end of Ṭughril Beg's reign Saljuq rule had extended into Syria. As much as the Saljuqs represented a continuation of power in the mould established by the Buwayhids, they were, nonetheless, progenitors of radical change. The most significant of these changes lay in the rejuvenation of a government bureaucracy, resembling that of the Abbasid court in its heyday before the Buwayhids, at the apex of which stood the office of the *wazīr*. In this context the rise of Saljuq power cannot be studied without mentioning the name of Niẓām al-Mulk (d.485/1092), the most influential Saljuq *wazīr* who in effect ran the empire under Ṭughril Beg's successors Alp Arslān (455–465/1063–1073) and Malik Shāh (465–485/1073–1092).

Several studies by Ann K.S. Lambton have comprehensively delineated the internal structure, economic and political, of the Saljuq Empire under Niẓām al-Mulk.[12] Among its several salient features, two are particularly relevant: the establishment and consolidation of a class of *amīrs* and a class of *ʿulamāʾ*. The rise of a self-conscious class of *amīrs* is connected to the implementation by Niẓām al-Mulk of a set of sophisticated policies governing the management of various sorts of *iqṭāʿ* assignments. Each assignee, usually a military man (*amīr*), supervised the use of *iqṭāʿ* land – at times, the size of an entire province – and, in turn, was directly accountable to the state finance bureau controlled by Niẓām al-Mulk. Apart from restoring a measure of stability, these policies were able to evoke an ideal of Muslim unity and territorial integrity as under the Abbasid caliphs in the preceding century – an ideal which found its most complete expression during the reign of Sultan Malik Shāh, and was elaborated around a delicate balance between a partly centralized and partly decentralized framework of connections between Niẓām al-Mulk in Baghdad and the scattered districts and regions in the empire. Furthermore, this ideal all too readily became an ideological banner behind which the Saljuq sultans presented themselves as champions of Sunni Islam – resulting in what George Makdisi refers to as: 'the Sunni revival'.[13]

This revival, in addition to other factors, drew its meaning primarily in relation to the fact that the Saljuqs seized power from the Shiʿi Buwayhids who, though antagonistic toward the Shiʿi Ismaili Fatimids in Egypt and North Africa, were lumped together with the Fatimids as being part of a usurping force for Shiʿi hegemony in the Muslim world. Thus the Saljuqs were now to reassert the ideals of Sunni Islam over and against the rising tide of Shiʿism. This reassertion expressed itself in a variety of ways, of which the most conspicuous manifestation was the cultivation of a class of Sunni *ʿulamāʾ*.

In the year 459/1067, Niẓām al-Mulk built a large *madrasa* in Baghdad that became known as the Niẓāmiyya, marking the beginning of what later developed into a vast network of Niẓāmiyyas throughout the empire. Our current understanding of the Niẓāmiyya network is predominantly shaped by the writings of George Makdisi, who has dedicated almost a lifetime of scholarship to studying its historical role and intellectual significance.[14] The comprehensive range and depth of Makdisi's research is at the same time striking for the original, and yet no less suggestive, interpretation which he elaborates on some of the major turning points in the intellectual history of Islam.

According to Makdisi, the intellectual genesis of the Niẓāmiyya can be traced back to the *miḥna* – the great inquisition (218–233/833–847) instituted by Caliph al-Ma'mūn (d.218/833) in order to enforce, as an official edict, the Muʿtazilī doctrine that the Qur'an was the created word of God, and thus to counter and suppress all the voices claiming that the Qur'an was the uncreated co-eternal word of God. Beginning with the failure of the *miḥna*, Makdisi posits the emergence of two divergent trends of thought: legal traditionalism (*fiqh*) and theological rationalism (*kalām*).[15] Traditionalism, as defined here, draws its sense of identity from the writings of al-Shāfiʿī (d.204/820) and the example of Aḥmad b. Ḥanbal (d.241/855), while rationalism is further consolidated and kept alive by al-Ashʿarī (d.325/937). Moreover, Makdisi endeavours to reconstruct the historic interplay between these two trends, yielding, in the process, valuable insights about the evolving conceptions of orthodoxy in Islamic thought. His analysis also sheds valuable light on the processes leading to the consolidation and designation of legal schools (*madhāhib*) around the teachings of prominent jurists (Mālikī, Ḥanafī, Shāfiʿī and Ḥanbalī); and on the complex and varied relationships between the emerging disciplines of law (*fiqh*) and theology (*kalām*). Building on this research, Makdisi's most original scholarly contribution perhaps lies in developing an explanatory framework for understanding, on the one hand, the excessive traditionalism, and hence anti-theological attitude, of the Ḥanbalites, while on the other hand, the development of an alliance, albeit uneasy, between the Shāfiʿīs and Ashʿarīs.

The Niẓāmiyya, for Makdisi, becomes emblematic of all the

aforementioned developments. He describes it as a college of law with a self-conscious mandate to teach the Shāfiʿī *madhhab* and to serve as a mouthpiece for Niẓām al-Mulk's religious policies. We are afforded a glimpse into these policies in the extant *waqf* deeds upon which the Niẓāmiyya was founded. A *waqf* is a charitable trust or foundation and its existence requires a *wāqif* (the founder of the *waqf*), who stipulates the conditions of use and administration governing the trust. Here, Niẓām al-Mulk is the *wāqif* and the *madrasa* Niẓāmiyya is instituted as a *waqf*. At the heart of Makdisi's scholarship on the Niẓāmiyya is his meticulous reinterpretation of the historical and intellectual implications of the fact that the Niẓāmiyya was instituted as a *waqf*.

The full import of this reinterpretation, which aims to retrace the lines of intellectual interaction and borrowing between Islam and the Christian West, is well beyond the purview of this study.[16] However, two particular strands in Makdisi's re-interpretation are of relevance for our purposes – namely, the reconstruction of the intellectual and political currents of the age in which al-Ghazālī lived and wrote the *K. al-Mustaẓhirī*. One of these strands relates to an examination of *waqf*, both as a law and an institution, especially in contrast to the *iqṭāʿ*. The other arises from an analysis of the stipulation in the *waqf* deed that the Niẓāmiyya should teach Shāfiʿī *fiqh* and *uṣūl al-fiqh*.

As regards the difference between *waqf* and *iqṭāʿ*, apart from the fact that one is a charitable trust and the other a revenue-generating assignment of land, there is also a further distinction arising from the fact that the founder of a *waqf* stipulated not only the conditions of administration but also the exact terms of its inheritance and perpetuity. The *amīr* in control of an *iqṭāʿ* had no such rights: every *iqṭāʿ* was subject to the Qurʾanic laws of inheritance and its legal status was specified by the prevailing opinions of the *fuqahāʾ* (jurists).

In this light, one can speak of a distinct law of *waqf*, conferring comprehensive private rights of patronage, independent of the sultan and caliph, upon the individual *wāqifs*. Niẓām al-Mulk appears to have taken full advantage of these rights in the establishment of the Niẓāmiyya network. The primary beneficiaries of the Niẓāmiyya were the *ʿulamāʾ* (scholars). According to Makdisi, the instrument of *waqf* enabled the schools of law (*madhāhib*) to be incorporated as professional guilds and thus, in turn, endowed upon the *ʿulamāʾ* the status of a distinct corporate body within Islamic society.[17]

Moreover, the processes of this incorporation appear, in part, to be connected with the continuing conflict between, on the one hand, the voice of traditionalism and, on the other, the voice of rationalism. Traces of this conflict can, according to Makdisi, be deduced from the 'Niẓāmiyya Baghdad Waqf Deed', of which only a fragment is extant. Among the several conditions in this deed, Niẓām al-Mulk stipulates that the Niẓāmiyya constitutes an endowment for the benefit of members of the Shāfiʿī madhhab who are Shāfiʿī in both *fiqh* and in *uṣūl al-fiqh*.[18] On the face of it, this stipulation comes across as tautological, since, beginning with al-Shāfiʿī, *uṣūl al-fiqh* referred to the fundamental sources or roots from which Islamic law (*fiqh*) can be derived, and thus al-Shāfiʿī's usage of the term '*uṣūl al-fiqh*' did not connote, contrary to its usage in the *waqf* deed, a separate body of knowledge as distinct from *fiqh* (positive law). This prompts Makdisi to ask: what then is meant by this particular use of the term *uṣūl al-fiqh*? He argues persuasively that by the fifth/eleventh century, almost two centuries after al-Shāfiʿī, *uṣūl al-fiqh* had evolved into more than just a descriptive term, and now carried the sense of being a legal theory or methodology; a theory which was incipiently present in al-Shāfiʿī's *al-Risāla* but which had, over time, been fleshed out into a system of jurisprudence concerned with an inquiry into the nature of God's law – His commands and prohibitions. This was unlike, and in opposition to, *kalām* (theology) which is concerned with the nature of God Himself. In effect, *uṣūl al-fiqh* is developed on a rationalist substratum, and though conscious in distinguishing itself from the rationalism of *kalām*, it is, nonetheless, infiltrated by the rationalist spirit of its opponent – thus leading Makdisi to define *uṣūl al-fiqh* as a 'juridical theology'.[19]

The labyrinthine character of the intellectual and political environment described here, constitutes the stage on which al-

Ghazālī was soon to make his entrance. Not much is known about al-Ghazālī's early life, though it is known that after receiving a standard, yet comprehensive, education in Ṭūs (with occasional visits to Gurgān), he enrolled in the Niẓāmiyya at Nīshāpūr in 470/1077 at the age of nineteen.[20] Here he was introduced to al-Juwaynī (d.478/1085), who could be considered the most learned scholar and Ashʿarī theologian of his day. In addition to studying the full range of the so-called 'religious sciences' (Qurʾan, hadith and the commentaries on both) with emphasis on *fiqh*, al-Ghazālī was also exposed to Ashʿarī *kalām*. He remained at Nīshāpūr until al-Juwaynī's death in 478/1085, then became attached to Niẓām al-Mulk's camp court (*muʾaskar*), establishing for himself a distinguished reputation in the eyes of Niẓām al-Mulk.[21] By 484/1091 he had been appointed to teach Shāfiʿī law at the Niẓāmiyya in Baghdad where, as we now know, he remained for only four years until 488/1095.

The drama, if you will, of these four years in Baghdad sits at the centre of our enquiry. The *K. al-Mustaẓhirī* was written almost at the end of this period, yet it was preceded by a significant amount of activity, all of which has a bearing on our analysis of this text. It is important to note that al-Ghazālī's appointment to the Niẓāmiyya in Baghdad coincides with the apogee of Niẓām al-Mulk's power – for that matter, the high point of Saljuq unity under Malik Shāh. Yet within a year of al-Ghazālī's arrival, both Niẓām al-Mulk and Malik Shāh were dead. The patronage of al-Ghazālī continued by virtue of the conditions stipulated in the *waqf*, but the advantage of Niẓām al-Mulk's personal influence was no longer to be had. Moreover, Malik Shāh's death plunged the Saljuq empire into a state of civil war. Several claimants for Malik Shāh's position emerged, among whom finally Berkiyāruq (*r.*487–498/1094–1105), Malik Shāh's son, and Tutush (d.488/1095), Malik Shāh's brother, were left to fight it out between themselves.[22] This conflict was protracted into a three-year war, in which Berkiyāruq proved victorious, assuming power as Saljuq sultan by Ṣafar 488/ February 1095. It should also be remembered that al-Ghazālī gave up his position at the Niẓāmiyya and left Baghdad nine months later in the same year. The civil war was a turning point in the life of the Saljuq empire. It marked the beginning of a gradual process of disintegration, thus endowing the preceding period of Malik Shāh and Niẓām al-Mulk with an image of Saljuq greatness.

A more important consideration for our purposes, however, is that of al-Ghazālī's official position on the civil war. This position can be interpreted around a varying set of images. First, there is the image of al-Ghazālī the *ʿālim* (scholar), carrying with it all the connotations attributed to the *ʿulamāʾ* at large. Apart from his position at the Niẓāmiyya, his tracts against the philosophers – most notably, the *Tahāfut al-falāsifa* – are written with a tone of authority indicative of someone who saw himself as a spokesman, if not a defender, of the *ʿulamāʾ*. However, being a recognized member of the *ʿulamāʾ* had its own particular set of challenges during this period; all of which were reducible to the fact that the role of the *ʿulamāʾ* was not a given, and the *ʿulamāʾ* themselves were embroiled in the process of defining, if not justifying, their status. This process of self-definition was, to be sure, not without its own complications.

It is this dimension which brings us directly to the political imagery applied to the *ʿulamāʾ*, and hence also to those images without which the *K. al-Mustaẓhirī* cannot be adequately understood. From this perspective, al-Ghazālī, like his kindred predecessors al-Māwardī and al-Juwaynī, is to be seen as a broker between the power of the Saljuq sultan and the authority of the Abbasid caliph. On the one hand, al-Ghazālī was only too aware that he was a beneficiary of Saljuq tutelage, while on the other he derived his legitimacy from the caliph's symbolic guardianship over the *sharīʿa*. Let us now turn to the circumstances around which al-Ghazālī was forced to negotiate a *modus vivendi* between the *de facto* power of the Saljuq sultan and the *de jure* authority of the Abbasid caliph.

Al-Ghazālī and the Abbasid Caliphate

By the time al-Ghazālī arrived in Baghdad, the pattern of assumptions and expectations supporting the body politic had already been subject to a fair amount of theorizing. Throughout history, formulations of political theory have been prompted by the desire either to legitimize or to change the contemporaneous political order. The genre of texts known as *siyāsa sharʿiyya* (juridico-political writing) was the channel through which political theory was formulated in medieval Islam, of which perhaps the most influential treatment is to be found in *al-Aḥkām al-sulṭāniyya* of al-Māwardī (d.450/1058), written in response to the Buwayhid seizure of power.[23] At the heart of the *siyāsa sharʿiyya* enterprise, to which al-Ghazālī was soon to make a contribution in the *K. al-Mustaẓhirī*, was the need and desire to keep alive a conception of caliphal authority in the Muslim community. The position of the caliph had been subject to historical change, and even though the actual role of the caliphate had become marginal and relatively impotent, in its symbolic role it continued to carry an ideological potency by which it served as a source of legitimacy for both the *de facto* holders of power and the *ʿulamāʾ*.

The post-prophetic history of Sunni Islam can be interpreted as that of a community struggling to preserve the ideals of the revealed message, while at the same time pursuing ways to fulfil the demands made by the revelation. God is seen as the all-encompassing source of these ideals, and God's demands are those expressed through His law. The meeting point for both His ideals and demands is the community: the community becomes the custodian of the ideals and at the same time provides the only plausible context within which His demands (the basis for the *sharīʿa*) can have any meaning. Moreover, the community is not some amorphous, abstract body, but in large part derives its identity vis-à-vis the authority of the caliph – who is perceived as the post-prophetic guardian of the community, and hence also of the *sharīʿa*.

Of all the areas of human life and conduct, the political structure of the community is one on which the Qur'an makes no explicit reference. In other words, the Qur'an does not contain a constitutional model for the organization of the community. Hence the *siyāsa shar'iyya* treatises could, and indeed did, have a relatively free hand in crafting their own constitutional ideas. From al-Māwardī onwards, there nonetheless existed a general consensus about the manner in which the *siyāsa shar'iyya* treatises were written. Apart from the fact that the caliph's position was vulnerable to being displaced by the power of the Saljuq sultan, al-Ghazālī in addition faced a situation where, because of the civil war, there was a breakdown in Saljuq control. The war created a vacuum in the power structure, thereby raising afresh questions about the future of the Saljuq dynasty and of the caliph's position in the empire. It was with the death of Caliph al-Muqtadī and the accession to the caliphate of the young al-Mustaẓhir in the early part of 487/1094, that al-Ghazālī was commissioned to write the *K. al-Mustaẓhirī*, a text which, to recall its full title, aims to extol the virtues of the Mustaẓhiriyya – or rather those supporting the caliphate of al-Mustaẓhir.

The continuing vacuum in the power structure weighed heavily on the position of the caliph, and al-Ghazālī, as a member of the *'ulamā'* attached to the Niẓāmiyya, could not but be affected by the situation. The civil war carried different levels of significance depending on whether viewed from the perspective of the Saljuq family, or Caliph al-Mustaẓhir, or al-Ghazālī. Each of these perspectives is embedded within a repertoire of expectations and apprehensions, reflecting the needs and desires motivating all these different actors on the scene. For the Saljuq princes, Berkiyāruq and Tutush, the struggle was for power and honour, fuelled by deeply-seated tribal impulses – impulses which had been characteristic of the Saljuq clan right from the beginnings of its wanderings, consisting of a 'survival of the fittest' type ethos. Leadership of the Saljuq clan, like that of all the other Turkic tribes, was always open to contest. Peaceful hereditary succession to power was rare. The reigns of Ṭughril Beg, Alp Arslān and Malik Shāh were by no means immune from internecine rivalry. Power within the extended Saljuq family was defined through the constantly shifting configuration of alliances and each alliance would spin out into factions aiming for the ultimate prize – chief of the clan. This, then, was the background to the conflict between Berkiyāruq and Tutush. The conflict revolved around an east-west divide: Berkiyāruq exercised control over Iraq and Khurāsān (the eastern part of the Saljuq empire) and Tutush had temporarily consolidated power over Syria (the western part of the empire). In between this divide there existed a whole chorus of less powerful factions, each headed by a prominent figure such as Malik Shāh's wife, Terkān Khātun (d.487/1094); Niẓām al-Mulk's successor, Tāj al-Mulk (d.485/1093); and one of Malik Shāh's brothers in Khurāsān, Arslān Arghūn (d.487/1094).

The unleashing of these internal struggles after Malik Shāh's death in 485/1092 must have been welcomed with a sigh of relief by the then caliph, al-Muqtadī (*r.*467–487/1075–1094), who had been under Saljuq tutelage since the time of Alp Arslān. So impotent had al-Muqtadī become that Malik Shāh, only two weeks before his death, had commanded al-Muqtadī in a ten-day ultimatum to abdicate and leave Baghdad. Malik Shāh had worked up a scheme whereby he had intended to install as caliph his five-year-old grandson Ja'far, who was born from an arranged marriage alliance between al-Muqtadī and Malik Shāh's daughter. Alas, Malik Shāh died before the ultimatum expired, giving al-Muqtadī, who remained caliph for another two years, a new lease on life. Thereafter his own appointed successor, al-Mustaẓhir, was recognized as the next caliph.[24] It is important to note that Malik Shāh's bid to bring the position of the caliph within Saljuq bloodlines was not the first attempt at such a fusion.

A similar marriage alliance had been attempted by Ṭughril Beg, and this time Ṭughril himself married the then caliph al-Qā'im's daughter. Once again, nothing came of it due to Ṭughril Beg's death shortly after the marriage.[25] The important point here, however, is that these attempts, along with the varied titles such as 'The King of the East and West', 'Reviver of Islam', and 'Commander of the Faithful', which the caliphs had been obliged to bestow on the Saljuq sultans, all point to their seething ambition and need for legitimacy.

The goal of the Saljuq sultans was to close, once and for all, whatever gap existed between the sources of power as distinct from those of authority. There is no more blatant a proclamation of this than in Niẓām al-Mulk's treatise entitled *Siyāsat-nāma* (The Book of Government), written in the form of a handbook outlining the duties and ethical responsibilities of a Saljuq sultan, and addressed to Malik Shāh. Niẓām al-Mulk puts forward a picture of the sultan as a sovereign monarch, modelled after the Sassanian example, who derives his power from God and is thus answerable only to God.[26]

By the time of al-Mustaẓhir's arrival on the scene, Saljuq civil strife had been running for almost two years. It is interesting to note that some of the chroniclers of this period project al-Mustaẓhir as a charismatic figure with an independent will.[27] An example of this independence, which is perhaps tantamount to asserting that al-Mustaẓhir had political ambitions of his own, has been recorded by Ibn al-Jawzī who claims that al-Mustaẓhir, upon becoming caliph, ordered the demolition of a prestigious marketplace in Baghdad built during the reign of Ṭughril Beg, which was known as Madinat al-Ṭughril.[28] Drawing on a wider range of historical sources, George Makdisi, in a remarkable article entitled 'The Topography of Eleventh Century Baghdad', elaborates further on the significance of al-Mustaẓhir's actions. According to Makdisi, the demolition of Madinat al-Ṭughril entailed also the destruction of a mosque (Jāmiʿ al-Sultān) connected to the market which had been built by Malik Shāh. Furthermore, al-Mustaẓhir had, after the demolition, intended to build on this site a wall bearing his own name.[29]

The implications of these deeds are rather telling. Al-Mustaẓhir, knowing only too well the history of Saljuq ambitions to occupy the office of caliph, could well have had his own ambitions to revive the power of the caliphate. Hence his action, which Makdisi aptly suggests was 'a move which demonstrates an increase in the measure of his [al-Mustaẓhir's] power among the Saljuqids who were involved in internecine wars for the succession to the Sultanate'.[30] Yet it would be unwise to overestimate the political ambitions of al-Mustaẓhir, due mainly to the fact that the civil war had come to a decisive end a year after his accession, at which time he openly recognized Berkiyāruq as sultan, although it is reported that he had backed Tutush during the civil war.[31] Complementing all this is the presence of the *K. al-Mustaẓhirī*, written some time during the first year of al-Mustaẓhir's reign, serving, among other things, as an important window onto the political climate of the period and the predicaments facing al-Mustaẓhir who, according to al-Ghazālī, commissioned him to write it and to whom it is dedicated.

However, the central figure in this window is al-Ghazālī himself. Questions about power and authority are at the heart of *K. al-Mustaẓhirī* which brings us, so far as the written word can, face to face with the workings of al-Ghazālī's restless mind. His treatment of these questions reveals fully the complexity of the dilemmas facing his society, while at the same time reflecting the dilemmas of an intellectual whose response to them is caught between the dictates of his own conscience on one hand, and the unavoidable demands of acting as a spokesman on the other. Al-Ghazālī had to think through, as had his predecessors amongst the *ʿulamāʾ*, how best to negotiate between the posture of an idealist and of a realist. Idealism, here, translates as the desire to return to an idealized conception of the community, in which the caliphate is once again whole and hence the source of both power and authority. Realism, by contrast, begins with an acceptance of historical change and has as its aim the preservation of stability and unity in the community so as to avoid the possibility of anarchy. For the *ʿulamāʾ*, as represented in the *siyāsa sharʿiyya* texts, and unlike the writings of the *falāsifa*, or say, even Niẓām al-Mulk, the challenge was not to justify one tendency to the exclusion of the other, but rather to negotiate and strike a tolerable balance between these two orientations. In *K. al-Mustaẓhirī*, the quest for this balance is woven around two strategies: firstly, the identification of those basic minimum requirements which need to be fulfilled, or enforced, in order to maintain the Islamic basis for the community; and secondly, carving out a political role and place for the *ʿulamāʾ* in the community. An analysis of the manner and degree to which al-Ghazālī succeeded in striking this balance will be examined in the next chapter.

Al-Ghazālī's silence on the civil war in *K. al-Mustaẓhirī* might be interpreted in several different ways. It could reflect an attitude, not uncommon amongst the *ʿulamāʾ*, of remaining neutral amidst the all too common inter-dynastic struggles, so as to appear non-partisan and thus avoid the consequences of having supported a defeated faction. This is not to say that al-Ghazālī was apolitical, but rather, on certain issues, as in this case, it was expedient for him to project himself in this way; or perhaps his silence reflects a deeper dilemma that he may have had in reconciling the prevailing arrangements between the Saljuqs and the caliphate. The types of questions confronting al-Ghazālī included, for example, whether the political reality of Saljuq power was there to stay, and if so, depending on the outcome of the civil war, how then to justify its continuing presence? And if it were to be replaced, what were the alternatives?

The silence in the *K. al-Mustaẓhirī* should thus be read as a posture that needs to be discerned between the lines, for only then can the implications of al-Ghazālī's theory of an Islamic government in this work be adequately understood. Regardless of the theoretical model that was elaborated, it is important to keep in mind that al-Ghazālī's theory was not a *creatio ex nihilo.* It was formulated within the framework and conventions of the *siyāsa sharʿiyya* tradition. By the time of al-Ghazālī, this tradition had become structured around a working relationship between the caliph, the Turkic sultans and the *ʿulamāʾ*. The caliph was conceived as the symbolic apex from which both the sultan and the *ʿulamāʾ* derived their identity as fulfilling functions delegated to them from the caliph. The Turkic sultans were popularly referred to as *ahl al-ḥall wa'l-ʿaqd* (those possessing the power to loosen and bind), while the *ʿulamāʾ* were referred to as heirs of the prophets (*al-ʿulamāʾ warathatu al-anbiyāʾ*), in the sense that they were an extension of the caliph's religious authority, the *de facto* guardians of the *sharīʿa*.[32]

This, then, served as the scaffolding on which al-Ghazālī sought to formulate a *modus vivendi* for the political tensions of his day. Yet all these negotiations represent only one side of the political coin influencing al-Ghazālī when writing *K. al-Mustaẓhirī*. The other side of the coin is subsumed within the latter part of the text's title: *Faḍā'iḥ al-Bāṭiniyya* (Infamies of the Bāṭiniyya). We will now turn our attention to the so-called Bāṭiniyya – who were they and in what senses were they, in al-Ghazālī's eyes, a threat?

Al-Ghazālī and the Ismailis

The term al-Ghazālī used most often for the Ismailis is 'al-Bāṭiniyya', which can be literally translated as 'the esotericists'. However, this translation does not adequately convey the range of pejorative meanings which al-Ghazālī had in mind when using the term. Beginning with the title of the text, it is here put forward as a term of antipathy – antipathetical to all that is implied by the term '*Mustaẓhiriyya*'. The title is framed in terms of a normative opposition between *faḍā'il* (virtues) and *faḍā'iḥ* (infamies). Hence, it is best to approach the term 'Bāṭiniyya' as a polemical construct. Like all such constructs, its meaning is conditioned by the presuppositions – the motivations and biases – of the polemical exchange in which it is used. In this particular case, the biases are those of al-Ghazālī as the self-styled polemicist on behalf of the Sunni caliph.

In order to analyse and understand al-Ghazālī's motivations, we need to step outside the polemical exchange as recorded in the *K. al-Mustaẓhirī*, and study the so-called Bāṭiniyya apart from al-Ghazālī's perception of them. This will help us identify more readily al-Ghazālī's biases in the text and also, more importantly, his polemical aims and strategies vis-à-vis the Bāṭiniyya.

The Ismailis whom al-Ghazālī referred to as the Bāṭiniyya, did not themselves use this term. At the time al-Ghazālī was writing his polemic, the Ismailis of Iran would most likely have referred to themselves as *al-daʿwa al-hādiya* (the rightly guiding mission), or as reported by al-Shahrastānī, as *al-daʿwa al-jadīda* (the new mission). The latter term, in turn, derives its meaning in juxtaposition to the term, *al-daʿwa al-qadīma* (the old mission), referring here to the Fatimid Ismaili *daʿwa* centred in Cairo. *Al-daʿwa al-jadīda* became a Nizārī Ismaili movement independent of the Fatimids, and was organized almost single-handedly under the leadership of Ḥasan-i Ṣabbāḥ (d.518/1124).[33]

Ḥasan-i Ṣabbāḥ's earliest connections with the Ismaili movement began as a representative of the Fatimid *daʿwa* in Rayy (northern Iran). By this time the Fatimid *daʿwa* had become an extremely effective organization, distinctive for the type of Shiʿi theology that it was propounding and for the far-flung pockets of loyalty it had garnered in Syria, Khurāsān, Transoxania and Sind.[34] Ḥasan's break from the Fatimid *daʿwa* arose out of a succession dispute following the death of the Fatimid Imam-Caliph al-Mustanṣir (*r.*427–487/1036–1094), the consequences of which had already begun to take shape during al-Mustanṣir's life. The Fatimid caliphs were concomitantly recognized as Shiʿi Ismaili Imams, and hence the succession dispute impinged not only on issues of dynastic power and continuity, but also on whether or not the successor was the legitimate bearer of religious authority. The sole criterion for legitimacy was that the successor be designated (*naṣṣ*) by the previous Imam. Al-Mustanṣir's designated heir was his eldest son Nizār (d.488/1095), but due to the rising influence and ambition of the Fatimid *wazīrs* and military commanders, Badr al-Jamālī and his son al-Afḍal, al-Mustanṣir's *naṣṣ* (designation) was allegedly bypassed and transferred to his younger son al-Mustaʿlī (*r.*487–495/1094–1101), who was married to Badr al-Jamālī's daughter. Al- Mustaʿlī's claims prevailed and Nizār rebelled by way of armed conflict, but was defeated. Ḥasan-i Ṣabbāḥ championed the cause of Nizār, of which it appears he first became aware during his year and a half long residence (471–473/1078–1081) in Cairo, at which time al-Mustanṣir was reported to have informed him that Nizār would be the next Imam.[35]

After Cairo, Ḥasan-i Ṣabbāḥ returned to Iran and began to consolidate a movement which, quite apart from crystallizing into an autonomous *al-daʿwa al-jadīda* and laying the foundation of what later became known as Nizārī Ismailism, also marked the beginning of a remarkable political organization, maintaining an existence out of castles and fortresses dotted throughout the Saljuq empire in Iran and later in Syria. From these strongholds the Nizārī Ismailis challenged Saljuq power and other subsequent powers in the region right up until the siege of the Mongols in 654/1256.

The *K. al-Mustaẓhirī* was written during the formative phase of Ḥasan-i Ṣabbāḥ's activities, just before al-Mustanṣir's death, and hence al-Ghazālī saw Ḥasan's movement as being an extension of the larger Fatimid rivalry with the Saljuqs. However, it is quite clear that al-Ghazālī's polemic, in spite of his many references to the Fatimid caliph in Egypt, was directed towards the activities and nascent ideas connected with the infiltration of Ḥasan's faction inside the Saljuq empire. Let us now turn our attention to the impact of this infiltration during this period up until the point when al-Ghazālī completed the *K. al-Mustaẓhirī*, which, as stated earlier, would have been sometime in the later part of the year 487/1094.

The political map of the Muslim world in the fifth/eleventh century had already lost its earlier sense of territorial coherence. Boundaries were constantly shifting in the name of different empires: the Ghaznawids were pushing west into India, the Almoravids were consolidating power in Spain and the Maghrib, and nestled in the centre were the Fatimid-controlled territories in North Africa, Egypt and Palestine – the juncture at which they met the lands of the Saljuq empire. It would not be off the mark to assert that the centre of gravity in the Muslim world of the fifth/eleventh century lay in the territorial and ideological opposition between the Fatimids and the Saljuqs. Both powers had imperial ambitions over the entire *dār al-Islām*. Fatimid claims rested on the authority of their Caliph-Imam in Cairo, and the Saljuqs asserted themselves behind the banner of the Abbasid caliph in Baghdad. The Baghdad-Cairo rivalry is a rich metaphor pointing to the two contesting visions of Islam. It was this contest that spurred al-Ghazālī into polemic. For al-Ghazālī, the entire Shiʿi Ismaili enterprise of the Fatimids represented the 'wholly other', with whom no compromise was possible. The Shiʿi Imam's claim to infallible authority challenged the very premises of the Sunni legal tradition, and hence also the *raison d'être* of the Sunni *ʿulamāʾ*.

Among the various challenges posed by the Fatimids, be it in terms of their naval supremacy or economic wealth, the most threatening, for al-Ghazālī, lay in the doctrines and activities of the Fatimid *daʿwa*. It would be rather reductive, if not misleading, to define the Fatimid *daʿwa* as a propaganda organization for the Ismaili movement. The range of ideas covered in the literature of the *daʿwa*, embracing some of the earliest expressions of Shiʿi theology woven around a Neoplatonic cosmology, and its application of an allegorical system for interpreting the Qurʾan and, by implication, the role of the Prophet and the *sharīʿa*, bears witness to a highly sophisticated and complex intellectual movement – a complexity which is further borne out by the historical evolution of the Fatimid *daʿwa*. The *daʿwa* began as an underground revolutionary movement, and though geographically dispersed it had the makings of a cohesive network from the latter part of the second/eighth century onwards. Thereafter it consolidated into an intellectual class within Fatimid society. At the height of Fatimid power the *daʿwa* had become an elaborate organization with the dual mandate of, on the one hand, administering and directing the religious affairs of the Fatimid empire and, on the other, of maintaining a strategic programme of conversion outside the Fatimid empire. In effect, the Fatimid *daʿwa* had two distinct faces, one belonging to the centre and the other to the periphery.

At the centre, which was Cairo, it was headed by the *dāʿī al-duʿāt* (chief *dāʿī*) who, in terms of authority and status, stood on an equal footing with the Fatimid *wazīr*. It was the centre which was responsible for systematic training and initiation of *dāʿīs*.[36] The periphery, especially in the lands of the Saljuq empire, consisted of clandestine groups of *dāʿīs*, who endeavoured to cultivate as wide an allegiance to the Fatimid caliph as was possible. The periphery was much more of a populist movement while the centre, by contrast, comes across as elitist. Its elitism is evidenced, rather ironically, by the fact that in Cairo and in Egypt as a whole there were no initiatives for mass conversion. Fatimid doctrines were propagated only within the *daʿwa* organization, and there also it was carefully disclosed through a piecemeal project of initiation. As a result, the Fatimid court in Cairo allowed Sunni schools of law to co-exist, and be applied, alongside a distinct school of Fatimid law which had been codified on Shiʿi principles.[37]

The situation was quite different in the periphery, and nowhere is this better exemplified than in the movement headed by Ḥasan-i Ṣabbāḥ. After returning from Egypt, Ḥasan spent almost a decade (473–483/1081–1090) travelling around the Saljuq empire, though primarily in western and northern Iran, consolidating support and loyalty for the *daʿwa*. The turning point is marked by the seizure of the castle at Alamūt, situated in the Daylamān region just south of the Caspian Sea. From this base at Alamūt, Ḥasan emerges as a public figure, initiating a policy of open revolt against the Saljuqs. It was this posture of confrontation and revolt that laid the foundations of what was to become the autonomous Nizārī Ismaili state right inside the Saljuq empire. Within a decade of taking Alamūt, the movement had spread widely across the neighbouring regions of Quhistān and Rūdbār, establishing their authority in small towns and fortress settlements on the pattern of Alamūt. More than the momentum of their territorial gains, it was the subversive manner in which they disrupted Saljuq power that attracted both fear and revulsion from the Saljuq establishment.

The image of subversion with which Ḥasan-i Ṣabbāḥ became irrevocably connected, was projected thorough the *fidāʾī*s (devotees) who would infiltrate the entourage of prominent Saljuq personalities with the aim of assassinating them.[38] Niẓām al-Mulk is alleged to have been the first prominent victim of the Nizārī *fidāʾī*s on 12 Ramaḍān 485/16 October 1092. Thereafter the bulk of the assassinations were of local Saljuq *amīrs* who attempted to resist or raid Nizārī Ismaili settlements.[39] By the time al-Ghazālī was to set pen to paper, Ḥasan's movement had taken on, for the Saljuqs, the proportions of an uncontrollable political menace which insidiously threatened the very fabric of their empire. For al-Ghazālī, this fabric was none other than the Sunni ethos of the empire.

Before Ḥasan's movement had become an actual political

threat, it was already perceived as an ideological threat by the Saljuqs. The earliest record of this perception is in Niẓām al-Mulk's *Siyāsat-nāma* (completed around 484/1091) in which an entire section is devoted to denouncing the presence of Ismailis inside Saljuq territories, referring to them as the Bāṭiniyya.[40] Niẓām al-Mulk's diatribe was built on the severe anti-Shiʿi attitudes contained in Sunni *firaq* (heresiographical) literature, of which the most influential writer was ʿAbd al-Qāhir al-Baghdadī (d.429/1037), the author of *al-Farq bayn al-firaq*. Al-Ghazālī's polemic was, in part, rooted in the assumptions and style of this literature, which sought to define the doctrinal basis for a Sunni orthodoxy. All who did not fit into the mould of *ahl al-sunna wa'l-jamāʿa* (people of the Prophetic tradition and the community/consensus) were given a sectarian label which, for the most part, became the basis for caricaturing their deviance, leading to either a legally derived charge of heresy (*takfīr*) or just plain demonization.

A sizeable portion of the *K. al-Mustaẓhirī*'s polemic against the Ismailis repeats this pattern. However, Ḥasan-i Ṣabbāḥ's burgeoning movement presented an additional doctrinal challenge, a challenge which required al-Ghazālī to conduct, in the *K. al-Mustaẓhirī*, an intellectual disputation (*munāẓara*), modelled on the style of *kalām* arguments, a style of argumentation of which there were many variations. In general, it involved the analysis of the opponent's arguments or claims, so as to examine the logical validity of the propositions on which they are based, and is conventionally written in the form of a dialogue with a hypothetical interlocutor. The doctrine which so struck al-Ghazālī, engaging him in a debate that continued to occupy him for the remainder of his life, was the Ismaili doctrine of *taʿlīm* (authoritative instruction or teaching).

This doctrine, of which Ḥasan-i Ṣabbāḥ was the major author, did not constitute a radically new doctrine but a terse re-statement – in the form of a logical argument – of the basic Shiʿi claim that mankind has always been in need of a divinely-guided teacher, and that after the Prophet Muḥammad it is only the Ismaili Imams who lay claim to such infallible authority. The force of this re-statement lay not so much in its content, but the manner in which it was formulated; consisting of propositions, each crafted so as to form a sequence of proofs, demonstrating progressively the inadequacy of human reason and hence the need for an authoritative teacher. The *K. al-Mustaẓhirī* is the earliest extant record of this doctrine and thereafter al-Shahrastānī (d.548/1153) is the next to cite it in his *firaq* text entitled *Kitāb al-Milal wa'l-niḥal* (Book of Religions and Sects). Nothing remains of Ḥasan-i Ṣabbāḥ's own writings on the *ta'līm* doctrine. However, al-Shahrastānī's citation purports to be a paraphrase from a text written by Ḥasan. Moreover al-Shahrastānī presents the most terse form of the doctrine, and the most widely quoted in Western scholarship, entitled *al-Fuṣūl al-arba'a* (The Four Chapters) – formulated as a doctrine composed of four propositions.[41]

Al-Ghazālī's account of the doctrine, beginning with the most detailed treatment in the *K. al-Mustaẓhirī* and then in four more works written against the Ismailis (of which two are no longer extant), never quite gets reduced to the terseness of al-Shahrastānī's four propositions. Nevertheless the overall import of the doctrine in both transmissions is similar.[42] In the next chapter, we will examine al-Ghazālī's version of the *ta'līm* doctrine and compare it with al-Shahrastānī's version. But now, let us analyse why al-Ghazālī was so taken up by this doctrine, leading him, on the one hand, to refer to Ḥasan-i Ṣabbāḥ's movement as al-Ta'līmiyya and, on the other, while recounting his intellectual and religious development in *al-Munqidh min al-ḍalāl* (Deliverance from Error), to place the challenge and impact of this doctrine as an autonomous category alongside that of *kalām, falsafa* and Sufism.

Al-Ghazālī's writings on the Ismailis were undoubtedly polemical through and through. Yet, especially in the *K. al-Mustaẓhirī*, the polemical confrontation went beyond the merely defensive or reactive, but could be characterized as a 'thinking through' of the Ismaili (or al-Ta'līmiyya) challenge. This 'thinking through' sought systematically to dismantle the fundamental Shi'i claims of the *ta'līm* doctrine, which, in turn, cleared the ground for a corresponding clarification of Sunni claims – claims which, as is amply borne out in al-Ghazālī's writings, were just as much in need of a 'thinking through'. The *taʿlīm* doctrine put forward a model of authority, the infallible teacher, which challenged the very foundations from which the *ahl al-sunna wa'l-jamāʿa* derived their identity. The latter has to continually reconcile itself to existence in a post-prophetic history, and hence to a conception of infallible authority (*ʿiṣma*) which lies in the past – and to which the Sunni community has to return by way of preserving and obeying God's revelation, and keeping alive the example of the Prophet.

The Taʿlīmiyya, who were equally locked into a post-prophetic era, proposed a conception of infallible authority (*ʿiṣma*) which, through the figure of the Imam, continues to subsist through history, functioning as a charismatic extension (not a substitute) of the Prophet's authority. The Ismaili Imam is thus contemporaneous with every succeeding community of believers (after the death of the Prophet). The community derives its coherence by recognizing and pledging allegiance to this authority, an allegiance which demands a 'turning towards' the living person of the Imam regarded as the unconditional source of *taʿlīm*. This stands in contrast to the Sunni posture which is a 'turning back' to the sources of authority of the past. Implicit in the Ismaili position is the judgement that the Sunni posture of 'turning back' is at best a fallible human appropriation or interpretation of infallibility. In other words, because the Sunni conception of infallible authority is justified through fallible means, the entire edifice of Sunni law and theology is judged to be intrinsically misguided.

The political, let alone intellectual, implications of the Ismaili position were only too obvious to al-Ghazālī. On the political front, al-Ghazālī was now confronted with the challenge of justifying the body politic of his time on premises that had to counteract the absolutist claims of the Ismailis. Al-Ghazālī had to put forward a defence of the Sunni order built on a vocabulary of ideals and not merely on realpolitik considerations as had been the tenor of previous *siyāsa sharʿiyya* texts. The Sunni caliph's claim to authority and power, apart from being burdened with disentangling his position from that of the Saljuq sultan, had to, in addition, be measured against the claims of the Ismaili Imam. On the intellectual front, the credibility of the *ʿulamāʾ* was at stake, especially of the claims they made on behalf of *fiqh* and *kalām*. The Imam in the *taʿlīm* scheme represents not only an alternative form of authority, but also an alternative source of knowledge. This body of knowledge stands in contradistinction to the Sunni traditions of *fiqh* and *kalām*. Claiming itself to be superior to individual reasoning, *taʿlīm* deals with certainties (*ḥaqāʾiq*) while *fiqh* and *kalām*, by contrast, have to resign themselves to conjecture (*ẓann*) or probability born of human reason.[43] Hence, al-Ghazālī had now to work out a defence for what, being a Shāfiʿī-Ashʿarī himself, were the sources of his livelihood in the Niẓāmiyya: the study of law and theology according to the Shāfiʿī-Ashʿarī school of thought.

Having reviewed all the major factors that were at play or that were directly or indirectly addressed in the *K. al-Mustaẓhirī*, it is now time that we turn to the content, structure and style of this text. The historical review so far has hopefully conveyed a sense of the complexity of both the circumstances and ideas which al-Ghazālī had to grapple with when writing it. It is a complexity that is borne out most clearly in terms of the issues surrounding the relationship between the Abbasid caliph and the Saljuq sultan, between Shiʿi and Sunni interpretations of Islam, and between the *ʿulamāʾ* and the body politic. At the centre of this complexity is al-Ghazālī himself, whose intellectual ambition and rigour, here and elsewhere, makes him one of the most articulate and engaged writers on the great questions facing the medieval Muslim world.

CHAPTER TWO

Anatomy of the *Kitāb al-Mustaẓhirī*: Content and Style

Every reading is also an act of interpretation, and the reading of a text, especially one whose author is dead, demands a particular type of interpretation. Short of getting entangled in a lengthy definition (as evident in the propensity for theory in contemporary literary criticism) of what I intend to convey by the use of the terms 'interpretation' and 'text', some cursory working definition will, nonetheless, be put forward.

'Text' refers to the written word, the organization and recording of which gives rise to certain common features between texts, the more prominent features being a beginning and an end, a style and a structure of the language in which it is put together, and a meaning (or meanings) of which it is a potential repository. 'Interpretation' is the property of the reader, it constitutes the basic relationship of the reader to any given text. The relationship is similar to that of a dialogue between two minds: the mind of the reader and that of the author. Interpretation, for the mind of the reader, is an effort to understand the author, and this effort varies from reader to reader, the variation being one of depth and comprehensiveness. However, the act of interpretation demands an engagement which, for all readers, begins with what I would call 'decipherment' and culminates in 'explanation'.

In decipherment the task at hand is to ascertain what the author has written, and how has he written – this falls within the purview of what is conventionally referred to as the style or form of the text. In addition, decipherment also entails an attempt to ascertain how the author actually understood what he wrote, regardless of whether he expressed that understanding explicitly or not – this aspect is conventionally referred to as the content or substance of the text.[1]

As with all conventions, the validity or even usefulness of the style/content (form/substance) dichotomy is open to debate. This distinction is a mental abstraction, and thus something that one would be hard pressed to verify empirically. In part, the difficulty presents itself as to whether style or content are irreducible categories; if so, can something called style be extracted from the text with the result that what remains is something called content? One plausible response to this question is to avoid it altogether, and begin, instead, by seeing this dichotomy as an abstraction. By thus accepting its limitations as such, one could, nonetheless, continue to draw on this dichotomy as a useful tool for analysis – useful in so far as it is precisely from this sort of thinking about a text that wider possibilities of interpretation are opened up.

It is at this point that interpretation expands and moves from decipherment to explanation. Explanation is connected to all the tasks which attempt to ascertain the implications and significance of the text of which the author was unaware, but we, the readers, due primarily to the benefit of hindsight, can probe as to whether the text represents an unconscious expression of a wish, an interest, a bias or a historical situation.[2]

In this chapter we will be working towards a decipherment of the *K. al-Mustaẓhirī*, in which the categories of style and content will be treated not so much as independent or mutually exclusive points of analysis, but as interdependent elements. The primary emphasis will be to read it as an embodiment of a certain set of arguments, and it is here, in the very idea of an argument, that the interdependence between style and content is most evident. In other words, as this chapter sets out to follow al-Ghazālī's arguments it will aim, among other things, to decipher the extent to which the content of these arguments is shaped by the style of argumentation in which he chose to develop, sustain and execute his arguments. Inasmuch as the preceding chapter attempted to define the ecology of the *K. al-Mustaẓhirī*, this chapter will pursue the task of identifying an anatomy of the text. This pursuit will encompass what has here been referred to as decipherment, and it will fall to the subsequent chapter to undertake an explanation of the text.

Al-Ghazālī's *Muqaddima*: A Justification

The *K. al-Mustaẓhirī* begins with a customary *muqaddima* (preamble) which consists of an introductory *khuṭba* (exordium): an explanation of the circumstances which led him to write the present work; a brief statement on the objectives of the text and a list of the titles of all ten chapters in the text (an equivalent, perhaps, to a table of contents). The deployment of a preamble such as this had become an almost standard feature of texts written in medieval Islam. Apart from its role in providing medieval Islamic texts with a common organizational style, the preamble as a convention forced upon medieval Muslim authors the requirement to justify their intentions for writing. Writing, thus, became a highly responsible endeavour; an author wrote not so much as an individual but as a member of a Muslim community – and it was to that, albeit reified, conception of community which al-Ghazālī had to justify himself.

An instructive way to decipher the manner in which al-Ghazālī justifies the writing of the *K. al-Mustaẓhirī* is to take notice of the different tones of writing contained in the preamble. There is a weaving together of three distinct tones: piety, loyalty and polemic. The tone of piety is introduced through the exordium, where, apart from affirming God's omnipotence and omniscience, God is thanked for having guided the author to righteousness and protected him from the errors of the people he calls the Bāṭiniyya:[3]

> Thanks be to God who has aided us to profess His religion publicly (*iʿlānan*) and privately (*isrāran*), and Who has guided us to submit to His rule (*ḥukm*) outwardly (*iẓhāran*) and inwardly (*idmāran*). He has not made us of the number of erring (*ḍalālan*) Bāṭiniyya who make outward confession with their tongues while they harbour in their hearts persistence and wilfulness [in their error].[4]

Having thanked God for His mercy and guidance, al-Ghazālī continues intermittently throughout the preamble to ask for God's help in sincerely fulfilling his intention to demonstrate the infamies (*faḍā'iḥ*) of the Bāṭiniyya and the virtues (*faḍā'il*) of the Mustaẓhiriyya.[5] Through this tone of piety al-Ghazālī justifies himself as a believer, with particular emphasis on the nature of his belief – a belief which seeks the path of truth (*ḥaqq*) and not error. Moreover, this belief, as al-Ghazālī was only too aware, takes on an outward expression through the act of writing and is thus attendant to judgement. This leads him to conclude the preamble with a reiteration of his desire to prove worthy of maintaining his integrity in this outward expression, his book:

> This is the sum total of the book – and God is the resort for help in following the thoroughfare of the truth (*sulūk jāddat al-ḥaqq*) and in treading the road of sincerity (*maslak al-ṣidq*).[6]

The tone of loyalty is not altogether separate from that of piety. It is, in effect, a further specification of his duty as a Muslim, which is here expressed in terms of al-Ghazālī's relationship with the caliphate, more specifically, with Caliph al-Mustaẓhir. Al-Ghazālī weaves this tone by employing the idea of service (*khadama*), stating that, while in Baghdad, he had been seeking for an opportunity to serve al-Mustaẓhir (interestingly enough, by way of fortifying the basis of his caliphate).[7] While still contemplating the matter, al-Ghazālī receives instructions from al-Mustaẓhir to compose a book refuting the Bāṭiniyya. The whole matter is thus elevated into a solemn duty towards the leader of the community (*zaʿīm al-umma*), and the fulfilment of which, according to al-Ghazālī, was nothing less than a call to:

> ... defend the plain truth and to stand up for the Proof of our Religion (*ḥujjat al-dīn*) and to eradicate the godless (*al-mulḥidīn*).[8]

In this way, al-Ghazālī not only charges the text with a sense of momentous significance (a call to arms), but, by implication, also takes on the role of a 'defender of the faith'. This defence draws its primary impulse from the need to uphold the authority of the caliph who, as encapsulated in the term *amīr al-mu'minīn* (commander of the faithful), stands as a symbol of the community.[9]

The above tone inevitably extends into a polemical one, fleshing itself out at almost every instance in which mention is made of the Bāṭiniyya. And what he has to say about them, at this stage, constitutes a foretaste of the more elaborate polemical engagement which will consume almost the entire text. The preamble attacks the Bāṭiniyya on three issues, each of which provides a key to what will turn out to be an elaborate argument later in the text. To begin with, there is the subject of the Bāṭiniyya 'error'. It consists, to put it briefly, in their repudiation of the belief that God appoints disagreement (*yajʿalu ikhtilāf*) amongst His believers. For as al-Ghazālī counters:

> ... despite the Bāṭiniyya unbelievers (*al-kafara*) who deny that God appoints disagreement among the People of the Truth, for they know not that mercy (*al-raḥma*) follows disagreement among the community just as admonition (*al-ʿibra*) follows their differing in ranks and qualities.[10]

The gravity of this error or its significance is, for the time being, left relatively ambiguous. Yet we can be assured that al-Ghazālī will, in no uncertain terms, return to this error. The other two issues are, in comparison, quite general. First, there is the imputation of 'godlessness', interlaced with accusations of their 'deception and dupery' (*ghwā'il* and *talbīs*): the Bāṭiniyya are presented as antithetical to the Truth.[11] Second, the Bāṭiniyya are represented as vacillating between the doctrines of the dualists (*al-thānawiyya*) and the philosophers. Apart from the pejorative rhetoric of these labels, al-Ghazālī is using them as metaphors to convey the nature of the polemical task that awaits him:

> For rare in the world is the man who, in the matter of fundamental dogmas (*qawāʿid al-ʿaqāʾid*), can independently undertake to establish proof (*al-ḥujja*) and demonstration (*al-burhān*) in such a fashion that he raises it from the lowlands of conjecture (*al-ẓann*) and reckoning to the highlands of certainty (*al-qāṭiʿ*). ... It is a weighty matter to the essentials of which the resources of the jurists (*al-fuqahāʾ*) are not equal because of the capricious tendencies regarding the fundamentals of religions (*uṣūl al-diyānāt*) which have appeared and become intermingled with the method of the early philosophers and sages (*al-ḥukamāʾ*). For it is from the depths of the latter's error that these Bāṭiniyya seek provision, since they vacillate between the doctrines of the dualists and the philosophers and buzz around the limits of logic (*ḥudūd al-manṭiq*) in their wranglings.[12]

Almost all the transliterated terms in the above passage will become springboards for al-Ghazālī's polemical aims. However, it is important to note that, though the subject matter in this passage touches on religious beliefs and principles, yet al-Ghazālī points out that the issues of this polemical engagement lie beyond the purview of jurists. This in itself is saying a lot, since the jurists are the *ʿulamāʾ* and hence the caretakers of the *sharīʿa.* Without delving too deeply into the varied implications of this assertion, we can perhaps tentatively read it as an affirmation of al-Ghazālī's intellectual individuality, a posture from which he is venturing into issues that have hitherto been unexplored by the *ʿulamāʾ*. This individuality is borne out in the way al-Ghazālī negotiates between the demands of piety, loyalty and polemic (a negotiation which he sustains through to the very end of the text). Al-Ghazālī's agility in this is demonstrated quite clearly in the first chapter, where he discusses the issue of method (*al-manhaj*).

Defining a Method

The aim and scope of this chapter are stated clearly enough in its title: 'The clear statement (*al-iʿrāb*) of the method (*al-manhaj*) I have chosen to follow in the course of this book'.[13] And as befits a statement, the chapter is short and to the point. In it al-Ghazālī defines his method in relation to three sets of criteria (which he considers applicable to all texts), consisting of a standpoint (*al-maqām*) on profundity and precision (*al-ghaus wa'l-taḥqīq*); a standpoint on prolixity and conciseness (*itnaban wa ʿījazan*); and a standpoint on reducing and multiplying (*al-taqlīl wa takthīr*).

With regard to all three standpoints, al-Ghazālī uses the term *al-maslak al-muqtaṣid* (middle way or *via media*) to describe the general approach of his method – hence in each standpoint al-Ghazālī argues for a compromise between the two alternatives. The significance here is in the rationalization for a middle way:

> So I have thought it best to follow the *via media* (*al-maslak al-muqtaṣid*) between the two extremes. I shall not leave my book devoid of matters apodeictical (*burhāniyya*) which the skilled researchers will understand, nor of rhetorical remarks (*kalimāt*) from which those who proceed by conjecture will derive profit. The need for this book is general, with respect to both the elite and the common folk (*al-khawāṣṣ wa'l-ʿawāmm*) and embraces all the strata of the adherents of Islam.[14]

Al-Ghazālī here conveys the sense of accountability and expectation with which he wrote. An accountability which is intellectual to the extent to which he realizes that he will be judged by his peers, the *ʿulamā'* (*al-khawāṣṣ*), whilst carrying a concerned expectation of being read by the literate community at large. It is through this remarkable ability of being both a popular writer while being an intellectual innovator that, in large measure, accounts for al-Ghazālī's enduring influence and uniqueness in the history of Islamic thought. However, one of the stylistic consequences, especially in his polemical writings, of this relentless balancing act between al-Ghazālī the populist and al-Ghazālī the intellectual, is the curious co-existence of a tone of emotive appeal alongside that of a more reasoned, critical approach. The populist in him is what fuels his polemical response to the Ismailis, and this at times makes him completely beholden to write what he feels is expected of him, thus compromising the overall intellectual integrity of his writings. This is strikingly borne out throughout the *K. al-Mustaẓhirī*, and, as such, this first chapter is not so much a theoretical statement about what, in contemporary parlance, would be called methodology, but rather a set of comments directed at his readership. The readership al-Ghazālī envisages extends beyond the *ʿulamāʾ* or the Niẓāmiyya sub-culture in which he taught and wrote, and hence he feels compelled to explain his method of writing, lest the *ʿulamāʾ*, unable to readily identify the conventional genre of this book (e.g. law, theology, heresiography or juridico-political), dismiss or misunderstand its significance.

The *Adab al-Firaq* Legacy: A Taxonomy of Exclusion

In the first half of the text, beginning from Chapter 2 and extending up to the end of Chapter 5, the style bears resemblance to the then emerging *firaq* (or heresiographical) genre of literature. One of the earliest and most influential examples of this literature in Sunni Islam is al-Ashʿarī's (d.324/925–6) *Maqālāt al-islāmiyyīn*, which was then further developed in the equally significant *al-Farq bayn al-firaq* of al-Baghdādī (d.429/1037). The Shāfiʿī-Ashʿarī stamp of the latter work explains, in part, why a good number of subsequent *firaq* texts were written by Shāfiʿī-Ashʿarīs, among which, al-Shahrastānī's *al-Milal wa'l-niḥal* was also very influential.[15]

Al-Ghazālī did not write a comprehensive *firaq* treatise in the mould of al-Baghdādī. Yet he was, without a doubt, influenced by the assumptions and the outlook of this genre. The heart of *firaq* writing can be described as a project to determine notions of an orthodox centre in Islam, and *ipso facto* to expose the existence of a heterodox landscape that differs from the centre. The difference is perceived in terms of the kind and degree of error and deviation which taints the inhabitants of this heterodox landscape. Of all of al-Ghazālī's writings, *K. al-Mustaẓhirī*, at least certain sections of it, comes closest to resembling the structure of *firaq* texts. The standard elements included a classification of sects with reference to the varied appellations attributed to each sect (*firqa* or *milla*); a brief history of the origins and development of each sect; and an overview of the beliefs and doctrines held by each sect. However the *K. al-Mustaẓhirī* differs from other *firaq* texts with respect to its intended scope. Standard *firaq* texts would, in very broad terms, define their objectives in light of the following hadith of the Prophet:

> Did not the People of the Book before you divide into 72 sects? ... And in truth this community will one day divide into 73 sects, of which 72 will go to hell, and only one to paradise.[16]

Hence it became conventional for a *firaq* text to encompass within its classification seventy-three sects (real or imaginary) of which the *ahl al-sunna wa'l-jamāʿa* was deemed to be the *firqa najiya*, 'the sect that is saved'.[17] The *K. al-Mustaẓhirī* does make reference to a variation of the aforementioned hadith (as had become common in *fiqh* and *kalām* texts), but in an altogether different context, of which we will say something more later.[18] It is, nonetheless, the more circumscribed focal range of the *K. al-Mustaẓhirī* that sets it apart from other *firaq* texts.

Chapter 2 begins with an examination of the varied nomenclature associated with the so-called Bāṭiniyya. Al-Ghazālī lists ten designations or titles (*alqāb*), of which three are connected with the conflicting divisions that had arisen in Shiʿism: al-Ismāʿīliyya, al-Qarāmiṭa – repeated separately as al-Qarmaṭiyya – and al-Bābakiyya. The remaining four are connected with the doctrinal positions projected onto the Shiʿi movement: al-Bāṭiniyya, al-Khurramiyya – repeated also as al-Khurramdīniyya – al-Sabʿiyya and al-Muḥammara. The final designation in the list is al-Taʿlīmiyya whose doctrinal claim is tersely presented as consisting of the following disputation (*mujādil*):

> Truth must be known either by individual reasoning (*bi'l-ra'y*) or by authoritative instruction (*taʿlīm*); but reliance on individual

> reasoning is useless because of the mutual contradiction of individual reasonings (*al-ārā'*) and the mutual opposition of the passions (*al-ahwā'*) and the disagreement (*ikhtilāf*) of the results of the speculation of the intelligent (*naẓar al-ʿuqalā'*): so recourse to *taʿlīm* and learning (from the Imam) is obligatory.[19]

It is this designation which according to al-Ghazālī is the most appropriate for the Bāṭiniyya of this era.[20] This is merely another way of saying that the text will predominately focus on this dimension of their error. Yet having unfurled the other designations, al-Ghazālī does not immediately shift his attention to the Taʿlīmiyya at the exclusion of others. At this stage he sets out to expose what he considers to be the range of *faḍā'iḥ* (infamies) connected with the so-called Bāṭiniyya. The exposure which is undertaken in Chapters 3, 4 and 5 does not refer to any one group in the nomenclature, but rather treats the Bāṭiniyya as a general, almost essentialized, category, whose identity subsumes many of the elements in the ten titles of his classification. With the exception of the appellation Taʿlīmiyya, the remaining titles constitute a collage, constructed so as to highlight major themes within which the infamies of the Bāṭiniyya are subsumed.

There are three central themes. First, the representation of the Bāṭiniyya as an organized conspiracy, fuelled solely by the desire for power and domination (*al-mulk wa'l-istīla'*).[21] This attitude is echoed in his description of, for example, the Khurramiyya or the Muḥammara, both of which draw on the then common stereotypes about pre-Islamic Iranian (traceable to the Shuʿūbiyya, pro-Persian and anti-Arab) antipathies to Islam. Although the Fatimids are not explicitly referred to in this context, allusion to the reality of their political threat, especially through the activities of their *daʿwa*, can be read in between the lines. The conspiracy theme is basically played out in Chapter 3, though, of course, references to it are strewn throughout the text.

The second theme is that of theological deviance, or, properly speaking, doctrinal innovation. What is emphasized here is not any one specific doctrine attributed to the movement, but the way in which they interpret basic Islamic concepts and doctrines – the *uṣul al-dīn*. This theme is explored later in the text when al-Ghazālī reviews Bāṭiniyya interpretations of God's nature (e.g. divinity: *fa-yataʿallaqu bi'l-ilāhīyyāt*); Prophetic missions (*al-nubuwwāt*); the Imamate (*al-imāma*); the Day of Judgement or Resurrection (*al-hashr wa'l-nashr*); and concludes with their views about the *sharīʿa* or, more precisely, the legal prescriptions of the *sharīʿa* (*al-takālif al-sharīʿa*).[22] References to the terms al-Ismāʿīliyya and al-Sabʿiyya carry, for al-Ghazālī, resonances of this theme.

Finally, the third theme is the alleged antinomianism of the movement (symbolized, in particular, by the image of the Qarāmiṭa). This charge develops from al-Ghazālī's summary of their attitudes to the *sharīʿa* (Chapter 4) and is further elaborated in Chapter 5 with a review and refutation of their interpretations (*ta'wīlāt*) of the Qur'an and Sunna.[23]

We will now examine the polemical strategies employed by al-Ghazālī in depicting each one of these themes. The term 'polemic' derives from the Greek word *polemos*, meaning war, hence writing a polemical text is to enter onto a battlefield. In contrast to an actual battlefield, the combat in a polemical text occurs through the use of language, and the corresponding tactical constraints are connected with the limits of language. These limits are experienced by all polemical writers, and the nature of the limits vary, at one level, according to the subject matter. For polemical writers the subject is the enemy and the enemy is addressed through an argument. Language here is thus at the service of two objectives: first, to represent the enemy; and, second, to develop and sustain an argument against the enemy. This, in a nutshell, encapsulates the nature of al-Ghazālī's enterprise in the *K. al-Mustaẓhirī*.

The first task that al-Ghazālī undertakes is that of representing the Bāṭiniyya. Representation in a polemical context carries its own particular challenges. On the one hand, the enemy is made to enter the text either through a faithful reconstruction of its own voice – by way of a hypothetical interlocutor – or through a relatively accurate paraphrase of its point of view. On the other hand, the enemy, is partly, or at times completely, invented by the polemicist. Al-Ghazālī partakes of both these options, and in fact the mixture of part reportage and part invention is common to all polemical texts. Al-Ghazālī's challenge, as for all other polemicists, is to ensure that when describing the enemy's point of view, it should be framed in such a manner as to carry the seeds of its own deconstruction or at least it should be amenable to a counter argument. The challenge connected with inventing the enemy, however, is to avoid overstepping the limits of plausibility; in other words the fiction has to have some sort of connection with reality and cannot be sheer fantasy. The earlier-cited themes of organized conspiracy, theological deviance and antinomianism are in themselves modes of representation, and each is substantiated through a strategic combination of fact and fiction.

As an organized conspiracy, the Bāṭiniyya are described in terms of an active missionary movement whose constituency comprises varied classes (*aṣnāf*) of disaffected individuals.[24] Such a description bears a general resemblance to what was then the character of the Fatimid *daʿwa*. However, as soon as al-Ghazālī launches into the details of the mission and the nature of their disaffection, it becomes quite clear that this whole section (Chapter 2) is essentially a crude, fictional caricature. Al-Ghazālī's aim here is to give the Bāṭiniyya a face, albeit one that effectively demonizes them. As such, this chapter is the most rhetorical of all, an example of which can be glimpsed in al-Ghazālī's classification of the nine artifices (*ḥiyal*) characterizing the Bāṭiniyya mission: (i) discernment and scrutiny (*al-zarq wa'l-tafarrus*); (ii) putting at ease (*al-ta'nīs*); (iii) inducing doubt (*al-tashkīk*); (iv) inducing suspense (*al-taʿlīq*); (v) binding by oath (*al-rabṭ*); (vi) swindling (*al-tadlīs*); (vii) deception (*al-talbīs*); (viii) denuding (*al-khalʿ*); (ix) stripping off (*al-salkh*).[25]

Through this schematic approach al-Ghazālī undertakes to parody the activities of the Fatimid Ismaili *daʿwa*, especially its missionary side wherein the *dāʿīs* would seek out individuals and invite them to a process of initiation and instruction. Al-Ghazālī sought to construct images of this initiation, images which had already been worked on by previous heresiographers when referring to what they regarded as the deceptive, insidious and conspiratorial character of the *daʿwa*. Al-Ghazālī's description is, however, embellished with a curious degree of detail. Apart from his fertile imagination, it is difficult to ascertain the sources for al-Ghazālī's descriptive details. The bulk of the information on the Fatimid *daʿwa* now survives in the theological writings of the *dāʿīs*, most of which concern themselves with questions of doctrine rather than the activities of the *daʿwa*. An exception to this are two early Ismaili texts: *Kitāb al-ʿālim wa'l-ghulām* (The Book of the Master and the Disciple) attributed to Jaʿfar b. Manṣūr al-Yaman and the *Iftitāḥ al-daʿwa* (Commencement of the Mission) by al-Qāḍī al-Nuʿmān (d.363/974).[26] The former is the only extant text which describes, in narrative form, the process of initiation which transpires between a *dāʿī* (the master) and a neophyte (the disciple). Echoes of this description can be discerned in al-Ghazālī's treatment, where, for example, the *dāʿī* begins the initiation with allusions to a deeper knowledge and the neophyte is, in turn, spurred on through degrees of deepening awareness and self-transformation.

Al-Ghazālī's objective is to parody the Fatimid *daʿwa*'s claim of possessing privileged knowledge in religious matters, and thus for al-Ghazālī this process of initiation is based on and culminates in a lie – a lie which masks a political drive in the name of religious learning. In addition, al-Ghazālī constructs a picture of the Bāṭiniyya as agents of unbridled deceit, who threaten the entire community of believers. Thus al-Ghazālī begins his description by stating:

> Let us now explain in detail each of these degrees, for in becoming aware of these artifices there are numerous advantages for the masses of the community (*li-jamāhīr al-umma*).[27]

And he concludes his description with:

> This, then, is the detailing of their step by step ensnaring of men: so let the observer consider it and let him ask God's forgiveness for erring about His [God's] Religion.[28]

Implicit in these statements is the message that al-Ghazālī

intends, through the act of writing, to strengthen the community's capacity to defend itself against the Bāṭiniyya, developing a defence against a siege to which the whole community is vulnerable, and which is at once both an insidious and an intellectual infiltration, amounting to nothing less than an organized conspiracy.

The charge of conspiracy becomes more articulately expressed in the second section of this chapter where al-Ghazālī describes the differing profiles of people who are attracted to this cause. He lists eight classes in all:

(i) those with weak minds (*ḍaʿafat ʿuqūluhum*) who are ignorant and stupid enough to believe anything; he groups these alongside those who are capable of deifying ʿAlī and thus capable of committing themselves to a lie (the subtext here is the equation of Shiʿism with heresy);

(ii) those who are seeking vengeance on behalf of their ancestors – pre-Islamic Persians – whose rule (*al-dawla*) they feel was usurped by the rise of Islam;

(iii) those with a sheer desire for mastery and domination (*al-tasalluṭ wa'l-istīlā'*);

(iv) those who seek to be a part of an elite so as to distinguish themselves from the masses (*al-ʿāmma*);

(v) those with intellectual pretensions whose reasoning, being incompetent, leads them to uphold beliefs they do not understand, but who do so out of servile conformism (*taqlīdan*) and with the illusion of superiority;

(vi) those who have grown up amongst the Shiʿa and the Rawāfiḍ and hence, *ipso facto*, share common interests with the Bāṭiniyya;

(vii) those godless philosophers (*mulḥidat al-falāsifa*) and dualists who, apart from believing that the revealed laws are man made (*nawāmīs mu'allafa*), have propped up the Bāṭiniyya cause with the requisites of dialectic and the prescriptions of logic (*shurūṭ al-jadal wa ḥudūd al-manṭiq*) – all of which is, of course, an empty shell;

(viii) those who are slaves to their passions (*al-shahawāt*) and find the constraints of the law unbearable. The Bāṭiniyya enable them to both justify and further their way of life.[29]

All of the above classes have the thread of bad faith running through them and it is this which serves as the source of their error, the clearest manifestation of which, according to al-Ghazālī, is in the corruption of their creed (*fasād ṭarīqatihim*).[30] This brings us to what I earlier referred to as the theme of theological deviance. He addresses this theme in Chapter 4, entitled 'On the Reporting (*naql*) of their Doctrine (*madhhabihim*), Summarily and in Detail'.[31]

Before taking up al-Ghazālī's treatment of this theme, let us first examine the nature and significance of the issues which are being handled. Variously through the text al-Ghazālī uses the terms *iʿtiqād*, *madhhab* and *ṭarīqa* in order to refer to what broadly translates as either belief, doctrine or creed.[32] Al-Ghazālī employed these terms as carrying almost synonymous, if not interchangeable, connotations. He applies them to both the Bāṭiniyya and the Sunni community, though one being false (*fasād* or *bāṭil*) and the other true (*ḥaqq*).[33] It is no arbitrary coincidence that, after having surveyed the mixed bag of motives fuelling the Bāṭiniyya, al-Ghazālī turns to the issue of doctrine as the site through which to transform the Bāṭiniyya into an ideological target. In other words, al-Ghazālī's polemic is directed not so much against the Bāṭiniyya as a body politic (a physical threat) but as an ideology (a spiritual threat) – the conspiracy is one of ideas. Hence terms such as *iʿtiqād*, *madhhab* and *ṭarīqa* are, for al-Ghazālī, ideological categories; they are not neutral but reflect expressions and instruments of power.

The history of Islamic theology has been marked by two distinct lines of development, associated respectively with the terms *ʿilm al-kalām* and *uṣūl al-dīn*. In summary, the term *ʿilm al-kalām* is connected with the rise of a method of argumentation, essential to which was a structured form of disputation (called *kalām*). The origins of *kalām* can be traced to the dissension generated during the caliphates of ʿUthmān (23–35/644–656) and ʿAlī

(35–40/656–661), crystallizing later into schools of theology, while the latter term, *uṣūl al-dīn*, is connected to a much more imperceptible development. The consolidation of the 'roots of religion' or 'articles of belief' (*uṣūl al-dīn*), has its historical genesis, according to George Makdisi, in the creed promulgated by Caliph al-Qādir (*r.*381–422/991–1031) known as *al-iʿtiqād al-Qādirī*.[34]

It is the *uṣūl al-dīn* perspective on theology which concerns us here, for it carries the ideological sense in which al-Ghazālī uses the terms *iʿtiqād*, *madhhab* and *ṭarīqa* – connoting, if you will, their power to determine orthodoxy or the lack of it. The topics of God, Prophethood, Imamate and Resurrection around which al-Ghazālī chooses to survey Ismaili doctrine, are among the central articles addressed in the Qādirī creed. Al-Ghazālī aims to demonstrate the irreconcilable degree of Bāṭiniyya deviance from the Qādirī creed on each of these topics.

Al-Ghazālī's transmission clearly indicates that he had access to some Fatimid texts (or at least second-hand transmissions from the original). However, once again, his survey is not faithful to the Fatimid texts but deliberately misreads them. He focuses primarily on the Neoplatonic strata of Fatimid Ismaili thought and parodies it as logically inconsistent and irrational. Beginning with the topic of God, al-Ghazālī at the outset charges them with a type of dualism, alleging that they uphold the conception of two eternal Gods (*bi'l-ilāhayayn qadīmayn*).[35] In support of this allegation, al-Ghazālī cites their use of terms such as *al-sābiq* (the Preceder) and *al-tālī* (the Follower); *al-ʿaql* (Intellect) and *al-nafs* (Soul); *al-qalam* (the Pen) and *al-lawḥ*(the Tablet). All of these are, in effect, technical transcriptions (or metaphors) used by Ismaili writers to designate the first and second principles in a Neoplatonic-inspired scheme of causality. Yet al-Ghazālī takes these terms out of context and alleges that for the Bāṭiniyya they represent two distinct, albeit muddled, dimensions of the Divine. And to further parody their doctrine, al-Ghazālī refers to their claim that the first principle in each combination (i.e. *al-sābiq*) is beyond existence and non-existence (*la yūsafu bi-wujūdi wa lā ʿadam*), calling it *tanzīh* (connoting absolute transcendence).[36]

Actually, this claim can be found in Fatimid texts, and several contemporary scholars have drawn attention to its originality in confronting the built-in challenge of contemplating the nature of an unknowable God in Neoplatonism. Al-Ghazālī's mocking and haphazard citation of it, however, was meant only to convince the reader of the Bāṭiniyya's baseless deviance.[37]

Al-Ghazālī concludes with a contrived and exaggerated tone of exasperation: 'This, then, is what is related of their doctrine, along with other matters more monstrous (*afhash*) than what we have mentioned',[38] adding that even if he went on to further disclose these matters they would all be denied – a consistent charge repeated throughout the text, referring to the Shiʿi practice of *taqiyya* (dissimulation). This tone jars so sharply with his more reasoned style of writing, that it points to a type of intellectual insecurity on the part of al-Ghazālī, especially since he avoids substantiating any of these exaggerated attacks. However, al-Ghazālī is agile as ever and claims that it is more important to focus on an aspect of their doctrine of which they make a public claim, namely: 'the invalidation of *ra'y* (personal reasoning) and the affirmation of *taʿlīm*' (authoritative instruction).[39] This shift, which would in fact mark a turn to an *ʿilm al-kalām* problem, does not receive detailed treatment until Chapter 6. Yet judging from the intermittent references to this problem, al-Ghazālī wants the reader to understand that it is this issue which concerns him most. Nevertheless, for the time being, he continues with the *uṣūl al-dīn*-based exposure and deconstruction that has been set into motion.

His review of the doctrines of the Prophetic missions (*al-nubuwwāt*) and the Imamate (*al-imāma*) are somewhat less accusatory, yet still disparaging, in tone. On *al-nubuwwa*, he recounts Ismaili theories about how revelation occurred to the Prophet: especially the theory of generation arising from the celestial interplay between the universal intellect and the universal soul, which in turn symbolizes the relationship between the Prophet and the Angel Jibrīl.[40] At the end of this section al-Ghazālī makes a revealing comment:

> These doctrines (*al-madhāhib*) are also extracted from the doctrines of the Philosophers on Prophetic missions, with some alteration and change. But we shall not plunge into refuting them. For some of them can be interpreted (*yataʾwwalu*) in a way we do not reject.[41]

Quite apart from associating the Ismailis with the philosophers, the above passage acknowledges the relationship between doctrine and interpretation, and hence implies something which will become clearer later in the text: that the Bāṭiniyya stand accused not for the act (or fact) of interpretation but for the kind of interpretation which they uphold.

Turning to the doctrine of *al-imāma*, al-Ghazālī begins with the claim that:

> Their Imam equals the Prophet in infallibility and knowledge (*al-ʿiṣma wa'l-iṭṭilāʿ*) and in knowledge of the realities of the truth in all matters, except that revelation (*al-waḥy*) is not sent down to him, but he simply receives that from the Prophet.[42]

Al-Ghazālī then continues to list the complementary roles and conceptions of the Imam vis-à-vis the Prophet in Ismaili thought. Among these he includes: the Imam as infallible interpreter of the Qurʾan and the Traditions; as silent (*al-ṣāmit*) repository of the spoken (*al-nāṭiq*) law of the Prophet; and as instrumental in the renewal of revealed law through succeeding cycles of Imams, modulated every seven generations and linked to the history of Prophethood from the time of Adam. Al-Ghazālī does not so much refute these doctrinal claims, but aims simply to mock as baseless the speculation on which they stand.[43]

In turning to eschatological matters, the polemical pitch is further heightened because the topic relates to a central and quite specific message of the Qurʾan. Al-Ghazālī had already confronted the Philosophers on this issue, where their denial of a bodily resurrection was, for al-Ghazālī, sufficient grounds on which to charge them with heresy (*takfīr*).[44] Along similar lines, al-Ghazālī asserts that the Bāṭiniyya deny resurrection (*al-qiyāma*) altogether, a denial that is not a blunt rejection but what, according to al-

Ghazālī, is rooted in untenable interpretations of resurrection. These interpretations include:

(i) resurrection does not entail a cessation of the world, as the process of generation (*tawallud*) will never finish;

(ii) resurrection as a reference to the emergence of the seventh Imam in the cyclical process of abrogation and renewal of the law;

(iii) the body decomposes after death and is thus not gathered again in the hereafter (*al-maʿād*), so that there is no physical Garden or Fire (*al-janna/al-nār*);

(iv) the soul, while in this world, is separated and in the hereafter returns and unites once again with the spiritual world (*al-ʿālam al-rūḥānī*) from which it originated.[45]

Al-Ghazālī summarizes the underlying aim of these interpretations as an endeavour 'to wrest literal (or exterior) beliefs (*al-muʿtaqadāt al-ẓāhira*) from the souls of men so that desire and fear might thereby be abolished' – this way he underscores the etymology of the term 'Bāṭiniyya' (interiorists at the expense of the exterior).[46] The Ismaili interpretation of *al-qiyāma* is cited as an example of this tendency. For al-Ghazālī this discussion marks an entry point into what will become the two central questions of his polemic: what are the limits of interpretation and hence at what point does it cross over into heresy; and what are the legitimate sources for interpretation?

These questions are approached in a variety of ways, and at this stage of the text they become embodied in al-Ghazālī's review of the Ismaili stand (or belief) concerning legal prescriptions (*fī iʿtiqādihim fī takālīf al-sharīʿa*).[47] This belief is unlike the four preceding articles of belief, and hence also the style in which he reviews this belief changes. The change is, in effect, a transition from an *uṣūl al-dīn* concern to an *ʿilm al-kalām* problem. Here al-Ghazālī introduces a hypothetical interlocutor and henceforth the text is written in the form of a *kalām* disputation.

Keeping in mind the questions cited earlier about interpretation, this section examines the related implications in more detail. He inquires, for example: if the unambiguous textual (Qurʾanic) evidence for *al-qiyāma* is denied, what then becomes of the letter of the law in the Qur'an? In other words, if, like the case of *al-qiyāma*, there is no limit to how many interior (*bāṭin*) meanings can be attached to legal injunctions, then law ceases to be law. For al-Ghazālī this constitutes the essential characteristic of Bāṭiniyya antinomianism.[48] Associated with this argument, and building on their interpretations of *al-qiyāma*, al-Ghazālī asks about the source of these interpretations:

> Regarding all their claims by which they are distinguished from us – such as the denial of the resurrection, and the pre-eternity of the world, and the denial of the resurrection of bodies, and the denial of the Garden and the Fire according to what the Qur'an has indicated with the fullest explanation in description of them, we say to them: Where do you know what you mentioned? From necessity (*ḍarūra*)? Or from reasoning (*naẓar*)? Or hearing it transmitted from the infallible Imam (*al-imām al-maʿṣūm*)?[49]

The categories of *ḍarūra* (necessity), *naẓar* (reason) and *taʿlīm* (authoritative instruction) henceforth become the central topics around which al-Ghazālī will frame his arguments. His immediate arguments following from the aforementioned passage serve as a dress rehearsal for the elaborately woven polemic that will unfold in subsequent chapters.

In response to whether their interpretation is based on necessary knowledge (e.g. self-evident fact), al-Ghazālī retorts:

> If you have learned it by necessity, then how is it that men with sound minds have contradicted you on it? For the meaning of something being necessary (*ḍarūriyyun*) and in no need of reflection (*ta'ammul*), is that all intelligent men share in perceiving it.[50]

In response to their claim of reason, al-Ghazālī states that for the Bāṭiniyya this would amount to a circular argument, since by upholding the primacy of *taʿlīm* they have *ipso facto* denied the validity of reason. As for their recourse to *taʿlīm*, al-Ghazālī asks: 'And what has called you to believe the Imam, who is infallible by your pretension, when he has no apologetic miracle (*muʿjiza*)?' –

unlike the Prophet. In effect, al-Ghazālī is asking what is the supernatural proof of your Imam's infallibility? Furthermore, he argues that if everything carries interior meanings, how then does one ascertain what the Imam has transmitted, since it, too, is presumably subject to an interpretation *ad infinitum*.[51] The polemic at this stage consolidates itself on two charges: on the one hand, that of circularity, and on the other of *reductio ad absurdum*. Al-Ghazālī's articulation of these two charges is encapsulated in the following charged passage:

> And at this point a man ought to recognize that the rank of this sect (*firqa*) is lower than that of any of the erring sects, since we do not find any sect whose doctrine is invalidated by that doctrine itself save this sect. For its doctrine is the invalidation of [the use of] reason and changing words from their [agreed upon] meanings by the claim of symbols (*al-rumūz*). But everything they can conceivably give tongue to is either reasoning or transmission (*naẓar aw naql*). They have invalidated reasoning, and as for utterance [i.e. transmission], it is declared allowable by them that one intends by the utterance something different than its agreed upon meaning. Hence there remains nothing to which they can cling.[52]

Over and above these charges, al-Ghazālī concludes this chapter by accusing the Bāṭiniyya of branding the Prophet a liar (*takdhīb*). This is how al-Ghazālī judges their denial of *al-qiyāma*, since for him the Prophet, being a mouthpiece for the revelation, is the reliable transmitter of this message. The gravity of this accusation is left somewhat ambiguous at this stage, its full polemical value still to be exploited in subsequent chapters.

In the next chapter (Chapter 5), al-Ghazālī examines the typology of Bāṭiniyya interpretations (*ta'wīlāt*), dividing them into two categories: those connected with clear literal texts and those associated with numerology. In brief, his aim here is to demonstrate the entirely absurd nature of their interpretations – a situation akin to intellectual anarchy where there are no limits or rules, just the sheer desire to destroy the sanctity of the law. This approach fortifies al-Ghazālī's continuing caricature of the

Bāṭiniyya in antinomian terms.[53] What is of interest here are not the examples of interpretations cited (their polemical handling or misreading is only too predictable), but his proposed strategy for refuting the interpretations. Al-Ghazālī's strategy consists of three methods: (i) *al-ibṭāl* (direct refutation – i.e. proving false); (ii) *al-mu'ārada* (confrontation – i.e. confronting a falsehood with another falsehood); and (iii) *al-taḥqīq* (verification i.e. defining the legal status).[54]

On closer analysis, the first two methods replay the charge of *reductio ad absurdum*, albeit with a modified set of arguments. The application of *al-ibṭāl*, argues al-Ghazālī, entails challenging the validity of every Bāṭinī interpretation by asserting that it, too, contains another, interior meaning and so on *ad infinitum* – such that all possible grounds for 'mutual understanding and communication' (*al-tafāhum wa'l-tafahhum*) are demolished.[55]

As for *al-mu'ārada*, it entails confronting a Bāṭinī interpretation imputed to be baseless with an equally baseless, yet contradictory, interpretation (or reading) of the same text. Essentially, al-Ghazālī is pointing out that since every Bāṭinī interpretation is derived arbitrarily, he too, can thus speculate in the same arbitrary manner, and as a result not only effectively silence them, but, by having reduced himself to their level, become more aware of their falsity.[56]

With the third method, *al-taḥqīq*, the arguments take on a different colour. There are two main issues at stake here:

(i) If, as is claimed, these interpretations are a product of the Imam's *ta'līm*, which is a privileged knowledge transmitted only to the initiated, what then is the status of these interpretations in law? Should they be concealed or divulged to the whole community?

(ii) If these interpretations were a secret (*sirr*) divulged by the Prophet (referred to as *ṣāḥib al-shar'* – trustee of the law) only to 'Alī (the first Imam), what then were the reasons for secrecy?[57]

As can be inferred, the arguments here are concerned with the legal and logical implications following from the Bāṭiniyya claims. In the first instance, al-Ghazālī is seeking to verify their contractual (or legal) value and in the second, their intellectual plausibility. Through a predictable, yet relatively convoluted approach, al-Ghazālī argues for the implausibility of the Prophet concealing anything in the first place, let alone transmitting something special to ʿAlī. Yet as regards the first issue, what is interesting is not al-Ghazālī's refutation (that Bāṭiniyya interpretations are baseless and possess no legal status), but the nature of the problem that he raises. It is a central problematic in the intellectual history of Islam, and is best captured through the following question: What is the relationship in Islam between ideas and the law? In other words, since it is the law (*sharīʿa*) which defines and orders the life of the community (hence reference to the Prophet as *ṣāḥib al-sharʿ*), then the Bāṭiniyya interpretations, by being void of legal meaning, are for al-Ghazālī 'but a departure (*khūrūj*) from [our] Religion (*al-dīn*), and an opposing of the *ṣāḥib al-sharʿ*, and a wrecking of all that he founded.'[58]

In retrospect, and having now traversed almost halfway across the text, the themes of conspiracy, theological deviance and antinomianism can be viewed as the conditions for exclusion. Exclusion here results from a transgression of what constitutes an ideal Muslim community intended by God and His Prophet. The chapters of *K. al-Mustaẓhirī* examined so far (Chapters 2 to 5) have in a taxonomic manner examined how and to what extent the Bāṭiniyya have fulfilled all the aforementioned conditions for exclusion. However, the climax of such a conclusion, being the unequivocal declaration of exclusion (*takfīr*), is here postponed. Al-Ghazālī now turns his polemical drive to attacking the *taʿlīm* doctrine itself. The ensuing analysis, apart from producing the longest chapter in the text, reveals clearly the issues and questions raised by the Ismailis that so obsessed al-Ghazālī and irrevocably influenced his thought.

The Place of *Kalām*: Reason and its Limits

Al-Ghazālī's refutation of the *taʿlīm* doctrine is far too nuanced an encounter for it to be interpreted in terms of any one single, clear-cut motive. Not only are several different motives at work, but they are all embedded in the very arguments employed by him. Hence a coherent understanding of al-Ghazālī's motives is only possible once we have carefully followed his arguments. As we endeavour to do this here, it must be stated that what follows is a synthetic review, a more detailed examination of each individual argument, though desirable, would warrant a separate study altogether.

The title of this chapter provides a general indication of what al-Ghazālī intends to accomplish:

> On the Disclosure of the Deceptions (*talbīsātihim*) which they uphold with their claim by means of [form of] Apodeictic Proof (*al-burhān*) of the Invalidation of Intellectual Reasoning (*ibṭāl al-naẓar al-ʿaqlī*) and of the Affirmation of the Necessity of Learning from the Infallible Imam.[59]

To put it more directly, al-Ghazālī wants to unmask and reveal the incorrect use made of *al-burhān* (logical proof) by the Ismailis to invalidate *al-naẓar* (reason), and also challenge their affirmation for the necessity of *taʿlīm* (authoritative instruction). As is commonplace in *kalām* texts, and this chapter embodies the very model of a *kalām* disputation, the gravity of the argument centres around definitions of key terms. Al-Ghazālī's refutation will itself be carried out through an inquiry into the definitions (so as to re-define) of *al-burhān*, *al-naẓar* and *al-taʿlīm*. The format of this chapter is structured around two sections: the first consists of an extended paraphrase of the premises and arguments contained in the *taʿlīm* doctrine, and the second, a refutation of these premises and arguments. That al-Ghazālī's presentation of the *taʿlīm* doctrine here is an engineered paraphrase is as much as admitted by al-Ghazālī himself:

> This is the accurate formulation of their proofs in the strongest mode of presentation – and perhaps most of them would be unable to attain such a degree of perfection in precisely formulating them.[60]

In other words, we once again return to the problem of

representation: the distinction between the *taʿlīm* doctrine *per se* and al-Ghazālī's construction of it.

We are introduced to the *taʿlīm* doctrine right from the opening lines of the chapter, where al-Ghazālī begins to list what he claims are its eight premises (*muqaddimāt*). He claims that the sum total of these serve as a proof (*dalīl*) that the Ismaili Imam-Caliph in Egypt is the one 'who knows the realities of things.[61] And that it is incumbent on all creatures to obey him and to learn from him'.[62] These eight premises can be summarized as follows:

(i) Truth (*al-ḥaqq*) is one and the false (*al-bāṭil*) is what opposes it; everything cannot be true, nor all false.

(ii) Hence there is an obligation (*wājib*) to distinguish the true from the false in both religious and worldly (*dīn wa dunyā*) matters.

(iii) As such, the attainment of truth must be known either through one's own individual reasoning (*ʿaqlihi bi-naẓarihi*) or through a learning process (*taʿallum*) from another.

(iv) Since the need for learning cannot be denied, there is thus also the need for an infallible teacher (*al-muʿallim al-maʿṣūm*) so as to safeguard us from error.

(v) Now, it must either be possible for the world to be devoid of this infallible teacher, or be impossible for the world to be devoid of him (since his absence would amount to a concealment of the truth and God would not allow such an injustice).

(vi) Therefore, the infallible teacher is the one who publicly declares (*al-taṣrīḥ*) himself as infallible.

(vii) And the (Ismaili) Imam is the only one claiming infallibility.

(viii) Therefore it is this Imam who resides in Egypt 'from whom it is incumbent on all men to learn the realities of the truth (*ḥaqāʾiq al-ḥaqq*) and to be acquainted with the meanings of the law (*maʿānī al-sharʿ*)'.[63]

Before moving on to an analysis of the central arguments contained in this version of the *taʿlīm* doctrine, it is perhaps appropriate to make a few general observations about the manner in which al-Ghazālī has framed the aforementioned premises. To begin with, they are ordered so as to give the impression of an interrelated set of premises, logically following one another, and sustaining, as it were, one continuous argument. But upon closer analysis, a justifiable distinction can be made between the first four premises where an argument is made to prove the necessity of learning from an infallible teacher. The four later premises set out to prove the necessary (and accessible) existence of an infallible teacher – culminating in a revelation of his identity. Both these arguments readily lend themselves to be classified as belonging to a specific class (or perhaps classes) of logic, but one thing is certain: al-Ghazālī has not ordered the premises in the form of a syllogism, though it is possible to construct one from them. I mention this here since al-Ghazālī, dissatisfied as he was with the undisciplined state of logic in *kalām*, was responsible for introducing a far more self-conscious and formal application of Aristotelian logic into the discipline of *kalām*. Moreover, it was in *K. al-Mustaẓhirī* that he (as we shall soon observe) for the first time utilizes the syllogism. Indeed, a leading contemporary *kalām* scholar, Josef van Ess, has asserted that it was the very challenge of the *taʿlīm* doctrine that impelled al-Ghazālī to use the syllogism.[64]

However, if we are to deduce a syllogism from the premises cited by al-Ghazālī, a strong formulation of it would read something like this:

There is a need for an infallible teacher;
Our Imam is the only one who claims infallibility;
Therefore our Imam is the infallible teacher.

It is important, nonetheless, to note that we have no record of the *taʿlīm* doctrine ever being formulated as a syllogism.

The transmission of this doctrine by al-Shahrastānī (d.548/1153), which purports to be an Arabic translation of a Persian text written by Ḥasan-i Ṣabbāḥ, is the one most often cited. This version is also not in the form of a syllogism, nor is it ordered around premises (let alone eight of them), but what al-Shahrastānī refers to as *al-fuṣūl al-arbaʿa* (The Four Chapters).[65] A freer, though by no means unfaithful, rendering would be to refer to al-Shahrastānī's transmission as consisting of four logically interconnected propositions or propositional arguments – which at one point he refers to as *al-muqaddimāt*.[66] The content of the first three propositions is subsumed within several of al-Ghazālī's premises, yet the fourth proposition does not correspond with any of his premises, and arguably gives the *taʿlīm* doctrine a different, far more subtle meaning than that found in the *K. al-Mustaẓhirī*. Al-Shahrastānī's transmission has been succinctly and elegantly captured in the following free translation of it by Marshall G.S. Hodgson:

(i) That for absolute truth, such as religion seemed to require, a decisive authority (an Imam) is needed, for otherwise one man's reasoned opinion is as good as another's and none is better than a guess;
(ii) that this proposition itself is in fact all that reason as such can furnish us with;
(iii) finally, then, that, as no reasoned proof could demonstrate who the Imam was (only that he was needed),
(iv) the Imam must be he who relied on no positive, external proof of his own position, but only on pointing out explicitly the logically essential but usually only implicit need.[67]

A more literal translation from al-Shahrastānī's text of the fourth and culminating proposition reads as:

> By the truth al-Ṣabbāḥ meant our need (*al-iḥtiyāj*), and by the one making known the truth, the one who is needed. He further said that through our need we come to know the Imam, and through the Imam we come to know the extent of our need.[68]

Apart from the differences of form and terminology (e.g. the elaborate conception of *need* in al-Shahrastānī), the crucial difference between this and al-Ghazālī's version lies in the way in which the relationship between reason and *taʿlīm* is portrayed. Al-Shahrastānī's version implies that recourse to the infallible Imam (hence *taʿlīm*) culminates out of an acknowledgement of the limits of reason, and not, as al-Ghazālī insists, the invalidity of reason. Since Ḥasan-i Ṣabbāḥ's original text is no longer extant, there is no completely objective way to arbitrate as to which transmission is more authentic.

There is further ironic twist in this intellectual genealogy, and this applies to the fate of the *K. al-Mustaẓhirī*. The contents became more popularly known through a summary and a polemical refutation to it written more than a century later by a Yemeni Ismaili *dāʿī*, ʿAlī b. Muḥammad b. al-Walīd (d. 612/ 1215). The title of this Ismaili response to al-Ghazālī is *Dāmigh al-bāṭil wa ḥatf al-munāḍil* (The Destroyer of Error and the Death of He Who Would Defend It). Henry Corbin describes it quite vividly as:

> ... a true *summa*, containing in its two volumes no less than 1250 pages (with 15 lines per page, and 8–10 words per line). Nothing is left out, and the tone of the writing is quite severe: Ghazālī is never cited as anything but a 'heretic' or 'one gone astray' (*māriq*). Here, almost a century after the end of the Fāṭimids, the Ismaili defensive has preserved all its vitality. The work itself is divided into twelve books (*bāb*). The first two make up a vast introduction, criticizing the intention of Ghazālī and the method of his work. The author cuts Ghazālī's text up into small sections, which he quotes literally in their entirety, and then responds to them, point by point.[69]

This ceaseless conversation between texts reflects what was stated at the very beginning of this study: the history of ideas is rarely ever simple.

Be that as it may, let us now return to al-Ghazālī's further elaboration of the *taʿlīm* doctrine. After listing the eight premises, al-Ghazālī focuses on the third (i.e. the attainment of truth must be known either through one's reasoning or through a learning process from another); and claims that the Bāṭiniyya *cum* Taʿlīmiyya formulated, in support of this premise, five additional rational and law-based proofs (*bi-adilla al-ʿaqliyya wa'l-sharʿiyya*).[70] Each of these proofs (referred to in the singular as *dalāla*) serve as supporting arguments for the premise: invalidation of reason entails the affirmation of *taʿlīm*. Al-Ghazālī recounts these proofs with force and clarity – this ability of his to enter into the shoes of his opponents reflects that very modern, almost liberal, side of al-Ghazālī's complex personality. The proofs can be summed up as:

(i) Whenever any point of view is affirmed, in it there lies also repudiation of its opposite, that which is upheld by your adversary. What is the basis for difference between the two points of view? Is it merely that each has reasoned differently? If so, each then resorts to claiming the superiority of his reasoning over the other, and thus there is no solid basis for distinguishing the truthfulness of one from the other. Either you acknowledge an authoritative source for your claim (i.e. *taʿlīm*), or you distinguish arbitrarily between the two points of view. And how is this to be done? By length of beard? Or whiteness of face? Or by frequency of coughing? Or by vehemence in claiming?[71]

(ii) When a judge seeking guidance is doubtful about a legal or rational problem (*masʾala sharʿiyya aw ʿaqliyya*) and claims he is unable to get to know its proof (*dalīlihā*), what do you say to him? Do you, then, refer him to his intellect (*ʿaqlihi*), the deficiency of which he acknowledges? This is absurd. Or do you say to him: learn the way of reasoning and guidance for the problem from me? If you say that, you have contradicted your affirmation of the invalidation of *taʿlīm*: for you have enjoined *taʿlīm* and made it a way (*ṭarīq*) – but this is our [i.e. Bāṭiniyya] doctrine (*madhhab*). Moreover, the judge will ask: what is the basis for you or anybody else to be my teacher? Who among you lays claim to infallibility?[72]

(iii) Oneness (*al-waḥda*) is the indication (*dalīl*) of that which is true and multiplicity (*al-kathra*) of that which is false. And oneness is an inherent property of the doctrine of *taʿlīm*, and disagreement (*ikhtilāf*) among them is inconceivable. But to men of *raʾy* (personal reasoning) there continually attaches disagreement and multiplicity.[73]

(iv) Everybody will acknowledge, from personal experience, that reasoned judgements change over time. Every reasoner (*al-nāẓir*) will attest 'how many times he has seen himself in one state, and his state has changed, and he believes a thing for a while and judges it to be the truth imposed by the reliable intellect, then there suddenly occurs to him a thought and he believes its contrary', and so on. All this just goes to prove that individual reasoning is unreliable in ascertaining the truth.[74]

(v) [The fifth proof], and it is law-based, is their saying: The Apostle of God (peace be upon him) said: 'My community will split into seventy-odd sects of which one will be saved'. And it was said: 'Who are they?' He said: 'The people of *al-sunna* [the custom] and *al-jamāʿa* [the consensus]'. It was said: 'And what is the custom and the consensus?' He said: 'What I and my Companions are now doing [saying and doing].' They say: And what they were doing was only following the *taʿlīm* as embodied in the Prophet's judgements concerning their disputes. So this proves that truth is in following (*al-ittibāʿ*), not in the reasoning of intellects (*naẓar al-ʿuqūl*).[75]

The eight premises and these five proofs combined constitute the framework of ideas which al-Ghazālī, having articulated it, now proceeds to demolish. Al-Ghazālī's refutation has itself the makings of a systematic structure. The refutation is divided into two sections, each one referred to as a method (*manhaj*).[76] The first method endeavours to establish the fundamental errors and inconsistencies in the argumentation of the *taʿlīm* doctrine; while the second method, broadly speaking, examines each one of the eight premises and accordingly subjects each to the class of arguments already elaborated in the first method. Al-Ghazālī's analysis can be encapsulated in terms of the following three questions which he puts to the upholders of the *taʿlīm* doctrine: (i) What is reason? (ii) Does our understanding of the nature of knowledge and knowing entail the invalidation of reason? (iii) Does all learning require the teacher to be infallible?

All three questions have been derived in response to the assumptions underlying the *taʿlīm* doctrine. Hence al-Ghazālī's strategy behind raising these questions is to clarify the error – intellectual and theological – in the claims of the Taʿlīmiyya. In addition, and perhaps more importantly, al-Ghazālī uses these questions as springboards to propose alternative definitions of the central terms used in the *taʿlīm* doctrine, namely, *naẓar*, *ʿilm* and *taʿlīm* itself.

Beginning with the issue of reason, al-Ghazālī replays the argument of circularity where he alleges that while, on the one hand, the Bāṭiniyya deny the validity of reason yet, on the other, it is clear that their doctrine has been formulated and ordered by way of reasoning (*bi-ṭarīq al-naẓar*).[77] With this assertion al-Ghazālī once again argues for the untenability of their claim that they have arrived at their doctrine through necessity and not reasoning. The untenability here is that if it issues from necessity, why then is it not treated as self-evident by all Muslims? Now, through a rather bold move, al-Ghazālī has his *taʿlīmī* interlocutor ask the following questions:

> And how do you know the validity of reasoning? If you claim necessity, you rush in to what you have deemed far-fetched, and you are embroiled in precisely what you have rejected. But if you claim, 'we have perceived it by reasoning', then how do you know the validity of the reasoning by which you have perceived that, since there is a dispute about it?[78]

Following from this, al-Ghazālī embarks upon defining reason itself, and though this move is connected to his polemical refutation, the pursuit of a definition becomes a larger agenda unto itself. Al-Ghazālī begins with the notion of reason as a tool or a method, referring in particular to the place of reason in geometry (*al-handasa*) where, for example, geometric principles have, through a process of reasoning, become encoded in formulae. The validity of the reasoning behind these formulae can be tested and verified by anyone who understands the rules of geometry; moreover the application of these rules 'afford knowledge of the conclusion (*al-ʿilm bi'l-natīja*) in a way that cannot be doubted'.[79] Such is the certainty that the premises (*muqaddimāt*) of geometry are self-evident (necessary) and are hence rooted in incontrovertible proof (*al-burhān*).[80] In support of this, al-Ghazālī cites the examples of the equilateral triangle and the equality of all lines proceeding from the centre to the circumference of a circle, referring to them as arithmetical cognitions (*al-ʿulūm al-ḥisabiyya*).[81]

The idea being hammered out here is that reason is a path to knowledge, the validity of which can only be ascertained through following it, much as one knows the right path to, for example, the Kaʿba after one has followed the path and reached the Kaʿba.[82] Yet in addition to this, al-Ghazālī is also narrowing the definition of reason (as *naẓar*) within the parameters of what constitutes a logical argument, that which involves organizing premises in order to arrive at an incontrovertible proof (*al-burhān*). His aim is to define reason as an autonomous method.

It is in this context that al-Ghazālī introduces the reader to the syllogism (*qiyās*), dividing it into two types or rather of containing two types of premises: absolute (*muṭlaqa*) and divisional (*taqsīmiyya*), or which he alternatively refers to as categorical (*ḥamliyya*) and conditional (*sharṭiyya*).[83] An example of each is cited. Of the former:

The world is contingent (*ḥadīth*) but every contingent has a cause.
The conclusion of it is: that the contingents [or: incipients, *al-ḥawādith*] of the world have a cause (*sabab*).
[Therefore the world has a cause.]

For an example of the latter type, al-Ghazālī accentuates the difference by rearranging the content of the first syllogism:

If it is certain that the contingencies [or incipients] of the world have a cause,
the postulated cause (*fa'l-sabab al-mafrūḍ*) is either contingent or eternal (*qadīm*).
And if it is false that it is contingent, it is certain that it is eternal.[84]

This personification of reason in the form of a syllogism enables al-Ghazālī to allege that the Taʿlīmiyya speak of reason without knowing what it means. Furthermore, for al-Ghazālī, the syllogism projects the desired autonomy of reason, an autonomy which is associated with the image of a neutral method at the service of knowledge, including knowledge of theological matters, as is borne out by the content of the aforementioned syllogisms.

Thereafter the text shifts to the issue of knowledge. Having defined the autonomy of reason, al-Ghazālī has now to qualify the parameters of this autonomy and hence distinguish himself from the philosophers, *falāsifa*, who were, by and large, advocating that reason has a limitless autonomy. Al-Ghazālī approaches this issue by arguing that knowledge is not homogeneous, and goes on to list three divisions of knowledge (or cognitions, *al-ʿulūm*):

(i) Knowledge which can be acquired only by hearing and learning (*bi'l-samāʿ wa'l-taʿallum*).

(ii) Intellectual, speculative cognitions (*al-naẓariyya al-ʿaqliyya*) in which 'there is not anything to guide to the proofs (*al-adilla*) regarding them. But for these there must be learning, not that one may blindly follow (*yuqallidu*) the teacher to them, but that the teacher may call attention to the way to them. It is thus that the intelligent man returns to himself and perceives (grasps) them by his own reasoning and so we do not need for that an infallible teacher'.

(iii) Religious and juridical cognitions (*al-sharʿiyya wa'l-fiqhiyya*) which cover knowledge of the law and about which certainty (*al-qaṭʿīya*) is not always possible. Thus 'one must be satisfied with conjecture (*al-ẓann*)'.[85]

Through the respective boundaries of this threefold division, al-Ghazālī attempts to integrate (or justify) the need for reason. The integration of this need was one of the central challenges confronting medieval Muslim thought, and al-Ghazālī's response, as encoded in the above divisions, gives us a cursory glimpse into the types of issues connected with this challenge. His first division concedes that there is a core area of knowledge which does not depend on reason, or rather that access to which is not arrived at through reasoning but through hearing and learning from the infallible Prophet (*al-nabī al-maʿṣūm*); the content of which includes, among other things, the apologetic miracles of the

Prophets, and what will happen on the 'Day of Resurrection and the circumstances of the Garden and the Fire'.[86]

In a rather subtle manner, al-Ghazālī reappropriates the conception of *taʿlīm*. In his version the infallible teacher is the Prophet and the scope of the knowledge involved is determined by the scope of what the Prophet has transmitted. Transmission becomes a key idea here, because even though al-Ghazālī asserts that the content of what is transmitted by the Prophet is a truth that lies beyond reason, we, he argues, nonetheless make use of reason in distinguishing whether a transmission is *mutawātir* (impeccable or sufficiently recurrent), in which case the knowledge is certain (*yaqīn* or *qaṭʿī*), or whether it is *al-āḥād* (a solitary report/report of individuals) in which case the knowledge is conjectural (*ẓannī*).[87] With this distinction al-Ghazālī further circumscribes his version of *taʿlīm* within the concerns and vocabulary of the *fuqahā'*, for whom the definition of conjecture was indeed of central importance.[88] As such, al-Ghazālī is, ingeniously, able to re-define *taʿlīm* and at the same time continue affirming the validity of reason, and this moreover in a manner which, indirectly, places the *ʿulamā'* (hence al-Ghazālī himself) as guardians of this *taʿlīm*.

In the second division (intellectual and speculative cognitions), al-Ghazālī returns to the notion of reason as a neutral method, the applied use of which is examined in the context of what he, to some degree tautologically, refers to as matters *al-naẓariyya al-ʿaqliyya*. The area of knowledge implied here is in all likelihood that encompassed by *ʿilm al-kalām*. Once again, al-Ghazālī refers to geometry and arithmetic as models where reason functions as a neutral method, and hence he argues analogically that *ʿilm al-kalām* makes use of reason in just the same way, though no mention is made of the syllogism. However, the key issue here is contained in al-Ghazālī's assertion that this use of reason is something which one learns from a teacher. In this regard, however, the teacher's role is that of a fallible facilitator, not someone blindly followed, and once the knowledge is acquired the teacher is no longer required.

The issue at stake is subsumed in the term *taqlīd*, a term which carried different shades of meaning, positive and negative. On the positive side, *taqlīd* meant following the opinions of a *mujtahid*, the best examples of whom were the founding personalities connected with each school of law. The posture of this following, serving as an important source of identity for each legal *madhhab*, differs from what al-Ghazālī had in mind with respect to learning the way of reason. The difference is dictated by the extent to which following in this context implies a reasoned submission to authority. As such, it is the degree of difference which accounts for the negative side of *taqlīd*, namely the connotation of blind and servile conformism, wherein it is seen as a posture antithetical to reason. Al-Ghazālī's aim here is twofold: on the one hand, he wants to equate the *taʿlīm* doctrine with the negative (servile conformist) connotation of *taqlīd*; and on the other hand, he wants to infuse the positive (legal) connotation of *taqlīd* with a sense of dynamic learning which accommodates the use of reason.

It is this accommodation of the use of reason to which he now turns in the elaboration of the third division concerned with matters *al-sharʿiyya* and *al-fiqhiyya*. Al-Ghazālī's central aim here is to make clear the relationship of reason to the law, and he accomplishes this through a three-part argument. The first part reiterates that since not all that is transmitted from the Prophet can be *mutawātir* (impeccable), recourse to conjecture (*ẓann*) is unavoidable. In the second part al-Ghazālī argues that the textual sources of the law are limited or finite in comparison to the unlimited number of incidents or cases requiring legal judgement, which, moreover, will continue to expand with the march of history. Both these factors lead him in the third part to conclude the necessity for reasoning in legal matters, and he refers to this reasoning as *ijtihād al-ra'y*.

Ijtihād can be broadly defined as the act of legal interpretation, but al-Ghazālī's intention here is to emphasize the individuality of this effort, denoting the sense of being a personal effort in the search for an opinion as to any legal rule. Without spelling it out, al-Ghazālī is, in effect, equating this effort with personal reasoning. Al-Ghazālī quotes the following famous hadith in support of *ijtihād al-ra'y*:

> Therefore, when the Apostle of God – peace be upon him – sent Mu'ādh to al-Yemen and said to him: 'By what will you judge?' Mu'ādh said: 'By the Book of God'. The Apostle said: 'And if you do not find [anything there]?' Mu'ādh replied: 'Then by the custom (*sunna*) of the Apostle of God'. The Apostle said: 'And if you do not find [anything there]?' Mu'ādh replied: 'I shall exercise *ijtihād al-ra'y* (my personal reasoning)'. Then he [the Apostle] said: 'Praise be to God Who has guided [helped] the apostle of His Apostle to what His Apostle approves'. So he permitted him to exercise *ijtihād al-ra'y* simply because it was impossible for specific texts to contain all the cases.[89]

Seen from this perspective, the term *ijtihād al-ra'y* enables al-Ghazālī to claim a role for reason which avoids what for him are the two opposing extremes of either the limitless autonomy of reason as advocated by some *falāsifa*, or the formal rejection of reason by the Ta'līmiyya. But most important of all, by referring to this role of reason, al-Ghazālī is inconspicuously turning the spotlight on the *'ulamā'*, for it is they who are the purveyors of *ijtihād al-ra'y*.

Al-Ghazālī's strategy so far has been concerned primarily with demonstrating the centrality of the law. Law becomes the vehicle through which the use of reason is justified. Furthermore, al-Ghazālī argues that the claims of the *ta'līm* doctrine demonstrate an ignorance of the law, and it is this ignorance which renders the doctrine invalid. As a way by which to reiterate this line of argument, al-Ghazālī returns to the thorny issue of the infallible teacher. He once again claims that the only infallible teacher is the Prophet, and the Prophet is here repeatedly referred to as *ṣāḥib al-shar'* (trustee of the law), thereby skilfully connecting the conception of the teacher to the law.[90] The nature of the connection is to portray the teacher as being dependent on God's law, and it is in the context of this dependence that al-Ghazālī acknowledges the specific and unique role of the Prophet in dispensing his preferred definition of *ta'līm*:

> Thus they [the Taʿlīmiyya] take *al-taʿlīm* as a general admitted expression, then they particularize it as containing the acknowledgement of the necessity of learning from the infallible Imam. You have understood what knowledge needs no teacher and what knowledge needs a teacher. And if there is need of a teacher, what is obtained from him is his method (*ṭarīqihi*), and he is not blindly followed (*yuqallidu*) in his own person – so there is no need of his infallibility. But when he is to be blindly followed in himself, then there is need of his infallibility. And [you know] that this infallible teacher is the Prophet.[91]

These, then, are the broad parameters of al-Ghazālī's arguments against the *taʿlīm* doctrine, the summary of which can be seen as consisting of three key elements: defining the autonomy of reason; integrating the use of reason; and establishing the basis for one's dependence on an infallible teacher (i.e. the Prophet Muḥammad and not the Ismaili Imam). The assertions of autonomy/integration/dependence provide the structural pattern for al-Ghazālī's subsequent detailed section on the *taʿlīm* doctrine, where he undertakes to refute individually each one of the *taʿlīm* doctrine's premises. The ground covered is quite extensive and intricate. The analysis here will be limited to some general observations about the central features of this refutation.

To begin with, the arguments in this section represent extensions of the broad parameters covered in the first section. Two sets of arguments stand out in particular. First, al-Ghazālī attacks the *taʿlīm* doctrine's essentialism with regard to its allegedly crude definitions of knowledge and reason. In response he sets out to construct further refined classifications of knowledge and reason. These classifications reflect, as it were, the varying levels of comprehension (or classes of people) in the community.[92] Second, he defends the unavoidability of conjecture (*ẓann*) in Islamic law. To be precise, he validates the possibility of disagreement (*ikhtilāf*) on some issues, and even though disagreement implies that some opinions may be in error, for al-Ghazālī this error is harmless in comparison to the grave errors and outright falsehood he perceives embodied in the *taʿlīm* doctrine.[93]

We notice, once again, al-Ghazālī's increasing reliance on the idea of the law as a framework within which he conducts his polemic. For example, when classifying knowledge, he emphasizes the importance of ascertaining the nature of the question being asked, and in doing so he transposes the characteristics of legal questions on to the general nature of all questions:

> Questions (*masāʾil*) are divided into what cannot be known by the reasoning of the intellect (*bi-naẓar al-ʿaql*), and what can be known with conjectural knowledge (*ʿilm ẓannī*), and what can be known with sure and certain knowledge (*ʿilm yaqīnī*).[94]

As for the issue of *ikhtilāf*, this was a central topic in the elaboration of *uṣūl al-fiqh*, and at its heart was the inquiry into the status of *ẓann* arrived at through *ijtihād al-raʾy*. Al-Ghazālī lets his defence on this matter rest on the weight of the following hadith:

> Error (*al-khaṭaʾ*) on details of legal matters (*al-fiqhiyyāt*) is legally excused by reason of the Prophet's declaration – peace be upon him – 'He who exercises *ijtihād* and is right will have two rewards; and he who exercises *ijtihād* and errs will have one reward'.[95]

However, he makes it clear that the task of *ijtihād* falls squarely on the shoulders of the '*ʿulamāʾ* of the law, who are the emissaries (*duʿāt*) of Muḥammad'.[96] It is on this note that we now turn to how al-Ghazālī, in his role as a member of the *ʿulamāʾ*, applies the law in resolving the problems connected with the Bāṭiniyya.

The Demands of *Fiqh*: Limits and Norms

Yet again, a reader of this text is introduced to a different style of argumentation and presentation, related now to the genre of *fiqh* texts. Al-Ghazālī's voice is now fully that of a *faqīh*, its tone at once decisive and practical, and the strategy to which it is harnessed resembles a prosecutor's attempt to clarify a point of law in court. There are basically two sets of problems which he sets out to analyse and resolve. The first, contained in Chapter 7 of *K. al-Mustaẓhirī*, involves an examination of the textual basis and legal status of Ismaili claims on the Imamate.[97] The second, contained in Chapter 8, involves an examination of the legal status and implications of certain points of Ismaili doctrine.[98] In the first case, the mode of examination is akin to that of source criticism; while in the second, it is essentially that of arriving at a legal verdict. Both tasks are subsumed within the term *ijtihād*, wherein at one end al-Ghazālī's concern with textual designation (*bi'l-naṣṣ*) embodies a process of legal interpretation. At the other end, his verdict is put forward as a *fatwā* (legal opinion), and as such represents an expression of *ijtihād*.

Beginning with the first problem – which al-Ghazālī refers to as that of *bi'l-naṣṣ* – he inquires as to whether any of the following assertions attributed to the Prophet are *tawātur* (unimpeachable):

> The Imamate, after me, goes to ʿAlī, and after him to his children; it will not go outside of my lineage (*nasabī*), and my lineage will never be cut off; and no one of them will die before charging his son with the commission (*ʿahd*);[99]

or:

> He whose Master (*mawlā*) I am, ʿAlī is his Master.[100]

Al-Ghazālī's response is that there is no evidence whatsoever to establish the *tawātur* of these textual designations. Moreover, 'if such texts were *mutawātir* (impeccably transmitted), we would have no doubt about them, for the Apostle's statements about designation would be of such importance as not to be passed over in silence.'[101] This argument is directed not only at the Ismailis but takes on board the basic Shiʿi claims for the Imamate. It is not without significance that al-Ghazālī's refutation is elaborated around the term *tawātur*. At one level this term is a construct used for evaluating the legal status of any text against the quality and quantity of the channels of its transmission. A primary condition for a text to be deemed *mutawātir* is that it be received 'through channels of transmission sufficiently numerous to preclude any possibility of collaboration on a forgery'.[102] On another, more conceptual level, *tawātur* becomes symbolic of the historical continuities which have shaped the identity of the

Muslim community – or, put differently, the standards of historicity which the community upholds in order to validate its beliefs and practices. Hence, the significance of employing the term *tawātur* lies not only in invalidating the fundamental source of Ismaili (and Shiʿi) claims for the Imamate, but as a means of implying that their claims lie outside the true history of the Muslim community. As such, for al-Ghazālī, the status of the Ismailis is one of deviation and transgression.

The characteristics of this deviation and transgression, with reference to specific limits and norms, are elaborated in the next chapter. However, al-Ghazālī concludes this chapter by clarifying, somewhat defensively, that he is objecting specifically to the claims for an infallible Imam and not to the office of the *imāma per se.* He is quick to emphasize that the Imam (referring here to the Sunni caliph) is not needed for the acquisition of knowledge but for practical or general administrative (*kulliyya siyāsiyya*) reasons such as resolving disputes, effecting harmony, defending Islam and so on.[103] At this stage the definition of the *imāma* is loosely framed, and a more elaborate formulation, as he himself reminds the reader, will be undertaken in Chapter 9. The aim here is to acknowledge a conception of authority as embodied in the institution of the *imāma*, and yet clearly distinguish an *ahl al-sunna wa'l-jamāʿa* conception of *imāma* from that upheld by the Ismailis.

Turning to Chapter 8, al-Ghazālī states his aim quite categorically in its title: 'Disclosure of the Legal Opinion (*fatwā al-sharʿ*) Regarding Them with Reference to Imputing Unbelief (*al-takfīr*) and the Shedding of [their] Blood.'[104]

Before proceeding to charge the Bāṭiniyya with *takfīr*, al-Ghazālī explains how such a judgement is arrived at, so as to stress the gravity of the issue, and to demonstrate that it is the outcome of a thorough investigation and not an arbitrary opinion. Al-Ghazālī was only too aware of how the term *takfīr* had been arbitrarily manipulated ever since the emergence of the Khawārij. He was thus keen to formulate a theory of unbelief, the value of which would not only safeguard *takfīr* from being misused but would serve as a key construct in supporting the idea of an orthodoxy – or, put differently, help establish its inviolable limits and norms. The strategy adopted in the *K. al-Mustaẓhirī* served as an early sketch for what would later become a detailed theoretical definition of *takfīr* as developed in his book *Fayṣal al-tafriqa bayn al-islām wa'l-zandaqa* (The Clear Criterion for Distinguishing between Islam and Godlessness).[105] A distinctive characteristic of this strategy was that it shifted the perspective of *takfīr* from a solely theological to a concretely legal problem.

In this chapter, al-Ghazālī treats *takfīr* as a legal term and begins by distinguishing it from other terms, so as to place it within a hierarchical scheme of judgement. *Takfīr* is juxtaposed with four other terms: *takhṭiʿa* (charging with innovation), *tadlīl* (charging with deviation), *tabdīʿ* (charging with innovation) and *tafsīq* (charging with sinfulness).[106] Though variations of degree are implied, al-Ghazālī does not spell out the variations but ends up referring to all four terms as being applicable to one general layer of Ismaili doctrine. These terms constitute a category unto themselves, a category which stands in contradistinction to that of *takfīr*. Examples of Ismaili doctrine which fall under this non-*takfīr* category include: upholding that ʿAlī should have been Imam rather than – or prior to – Abu Bakr, ʿUmar and ʿUthmān; and attributing the quality of infallibility (*ʿiṣma*) to their Imam.[107]

Al-Ghazālī interprets the first claim as a contravention of the principle of 'consensus' (*kharq al-ijmāʿ*), and since *ijmāʿ* is recognized as a source of law, this claim represents a fundamental deviation, yet not fundamental enough to warrant the charge of *takfīr*, as al-Ghazālī the *faqīh* states: 'It is not clear to us that the contravener of consensus is a *kāfir* (unbeliever).'[108] This is perhaps an indication of how *takfīr* as a legal problem was still a relatively uncharted area. However, al-Ghazālī is hinting that *takfīr* is or should be associated with clear evidence. In this respect the claim of infallibility also falls short of *takfīr*, asserting instead, again without delving deeply, that it is simply a matter of error (*takhṭi'a*).[109] This admission is rather revealing as it puts into proper perspective the significance of al-Ghazālī's refutation of the *taʿlīm* doctrine, the cornerstone of which is the existence of an infallible teacher. The above admission implies that the errors of the *taʿlīm* doctrine do not in themselves infringe on the *uṣūl*, be that of *dīn* or *fiqh*.

Al-Ghazālī's connection of *takfīr* with this specific sense of infringement focuses further his pursuit to arrive at a legalistic rationale for *takfīr*. Hence it is not surprising that al-Ghazālī returns to the figure of the Prophet in his status as *ṣāḥib al-sharʿ*, positing him not only as the guardian of *fiqh* but the mouthpiece for the *uṣūl al-dīn*. And it is in this context that al-Ghazālī introduces the term *takdhīb* – a charge applicable to anyone who makes the Prophet out to be a liar, arising from any claim that contradicts the message delivered by the Prophet.[110] *Takdhīb* is put forward as the primary pre-condition for *takfīr*. Al-Ghazālī next turns his attention to the Ismaili interpretations of the *uṣūl al-dīn* reviewed in Chapter 4, and asserts unequivocally that their denial of a bodily resurrection (and a physical garden and a fire in the afterlife) is a clear case in point of *takdhīb* and warrants the charge of *takfīr*:

> What we settle for and hold positively is the charging with unbelief (*takfīr*) of anyone who holds any of that, because it is plainly giving the lie (*takdhīb*) to the Trustee of the Law (*li-ṣāḥib al-sharʿ*) and to all the words of the Qur'an from their first to their last. Descriptions of the Garden and the Fire are in plain terms plainly intended – so what such a person holds is *takdhīb*, not *ta'wīl*.[111]

Following from the above passage al-Ghazālī labours to make the distinction that it is not the exercise of *ta'wīl* in itself that renders the Bāṭiniyya guilty of *kufr*, but it is due to the kind of *ta'wīl* that they uphold. For al-Ghazālī this kind of interpretation ceases to be *ta'wīl* as practised in *kalām* (as to the nature of God's attributes), and is hence nothing but *takdhīb*.[112] However, he cuts this discussion short by claiming, rather enigmatically, that this subject (presumably *ta'wīl*) entails entering into 'the mysteries of religion' (*asrār al-dīn*), further discussion of which would detract from the 'more important aims (*maqāṣid*) of this book'.[113] Though this statement is unclear, it appears that the detraction al-Ghazālī has in mind is the mixing up of *kalām* issues with that of *fiqh*-based arguments. It is also interesting to note that in his later works such as *Mishkāt al-anwār* (The Niche of Lights) and *Iḥyā' 'ulūm al-dīn* (The Revivification of the Religious Sciences), al-Ghazali takes on a far more open and flexible approach to *ta'wīl*, and in fact these contain passages where he even alludes to the metaphorical nature of resurrection.

The ambiguities around the issue of *ta'wīl* are completely defused as al-Ghazālī shifts his attention into specifying the legal consequences associated with the *fatwā* of *takfīr*. He is now involved in passing a legal ruling, much as a *muftī* would, and the key term in this endeavour is that of *aḥkām* (legal statutes).[114] The *ṣāḥib* of each and every individual within the Bāṭiniyya is decreed to be that of a *murtadd* (apostate), thereby subjecting the Bāṭiniyya to the most direct form of exclusion. Moreover, since the phenomenon of apostasy is intimately interwoven with the history of the early Muslim community, al-Ghazālī is here appealing to atavistic impulses. The Bāṭiniyya became associated with archetypes of betrayal and corruption, the threat of which is clearly referred to in the Qur'an and Sunna.

By framing the problem in terms of the legal management of apostasy, al-Ghazālī is implicitly personifying the law as a guardian of the truth.[115] Although there is no evidence in the text, it is quite likely that his recourse to the vocabulary of apostasy is reflective of the very real (or so perceived) political threat exercised by Ḥasan-i Ṣabbāḥ's burgeoning Ismaili movement in Iran. As such, al-Ghazālī handles the law as an instrument of power, the efficacy of which, having effectively taken care of the Bāṭiniyya, is going to now be used in justifying the authority and status of Caliph al-Mustaẓhir.

The Body Politic in Medieval Islam: Justification and Narcissism

Al-Ghazālī concludes his text with what he would want to be perceived as the culminating *raison d'être* of his efforts, namely a demonstration of the *faḍā'il-mustaẓhiriyya* (virtues of the

Mustaẓhiriyya). This demonstration is accomplished through two distinct, yet interrelated, styles of presentation: that of a *siyāsa sharʿiyya* (juridico-political) text in Chapter 9, and a rendition of a *naṣīḥat al-mulūk* (mirror for princes) or *fürstenspiegel* text in Chapter 10.

For several Western scholars, in particular Erwin Rosenthal, Ann Lambton and Carole Hillenbrand, the primary significance of the *Kitāb al-Mustaẓhirī* lies in the so-called theory of government which it expounds. As a result, these scholars have for the most part approached the *K. al-Mustaẓhirī* strictly as a *siyāsa sharʿiyya* text, with a special focus on comparing al-Ghazālī's political views in it (specifically Chapter 9) with those subsequently elaborated in his *Kitāb al-Iqtiṣād fi'l-iʿtiqād* (Moderation in Belief) and in the multi-volume *Iḥyāʾ ʿulūm al-dīn.*[116] Even Henri Laoust's comprehensive study, *La Politique de Gazālī*, which takes a relatively broader view of the *Kitāb al-Mustaẓhirī*, is still concerned primarily with assessing the chronological development of al-Ghazālī's political thought.[117]

This developmental and *siyāsa sharʿiyya*-specific perspective has yielded some extremely valuable insights for understanding the historical conditions which have influenced al-Ghazālī's writings, the most thorough review of which is to be found in Carole Hillenbrand's article 'Islamic Orthodoxy or Realpolitik? Al-Ghazālī's Views on Government'. However, by reading the *K. al-Mustaẓhirī* through what is at once a broad historical and yet a narrow thematic approach, these studies have glossed over or left unexplained some of the salient features in al-Ghazālī's definition of the caliphate. Through an examination of these salient features my aim is to demonstrate the extent to which the contents of the *siyāsa sharʿiyya* section in the *K. al-Mustaẓhirī* embodied a response to the perceived intellectual and political threat of the Fatimid Ismailis, whom al-Ghazālī continued to designate as the Bāṭiniyya, and hence to argue that this section cannot, as has hitherto been the case, be examined in isolation – or rather disconnected from the overall fabric of the text. This examination will also argue for the plausibility of a different explanation of why, apart from the Bāṭiniyya factor, the views in the *K. al-Mustaẓhirī* differed from those which he subsequently elaborated.

Before turning to the text, it might be appropriate to make some general observations about the objectives which lay behind the *siyāsa sharʿiyya* genre, so as to provide a background to the assumptions, stated and unstated, with which al-Ghazālī had to wrestle when writing the *K. al-Mustaẓhirī*. Some of the most insightful research in this area is contained in the masterly articles written by Sir Hamilton A.R. Gibb, from which the following passage serves as a fertile point of departure for our purposes:

> ... Sunni political theory was, in fact, only the rationalization of the history of the community. Without precedents, no theory; and all the imposing fabric of interpretation of the sources is merely the *post eventum* justification of the precedents which have been ratified by *ijmāʿ*.[118]

Gibb arrives at the above conclusion by way of a detailed analysis of al-Māwardī's *al-Aḥkām al-sulṭāniyya*, which, as mentioned earlier, is considered to have set the model for subsequent *siyāsa sharʿiyya* texts. This model, in addition to its Shāfiʿī-Ashʿarī, character features two dominant impulses: first, the justification of the caliph's authority in the face of the Buwayhid sultan's *de facto* power; and second, the interpretation of the Islamic body politic as embodying the ideal of historical continuity in the face of changing circumstances. Hence the 'rationalization' to which Gibb refers is, on one hand, directed at a *legal* ideal, concerned with defining the status of the caliph; on the other hand, there is an endeavour to articulate a *political* ideal of which the Muslim community is at once a witness and a mouthpiece. It is the delicate balancing between these two ideals (legal and political) – ensuring that they feed off each other while remaining distinct – that becomes the key objective of *siyāsa sharʿiyya* texts after al-Māwardī. Moreover, it is the interplay between both these ideals that forms the framework around which al-Ghazālī composed Chapter 9 of the *K. al-Mustaẓhirī*.

Al-Ghazālī begins the chapter with a clear emphasis on the legal ideal, as expressed in the wording of the chapter's title:

On the Establishment of the Legal Demonstrations (*al-barāhīn al-sharʿiyya*) that the Imam charged with the Truth whom all Men are Bound to obey in this Age of Ours is the Imam al-Mustaẓhir Billāh.[119]

By the use of the term *al-barāhīn al-sharʿiyya,* al-Ghazālī intends to give the impression that the basis (or proof) of the caliphate is clearly contained in the law, when in fact, as mentioned earlier, both the Qurʾan and the Sunna are silent about matters pertaining to constitutional law. What passes as Islamic constitutional law is essentially a product of *ijtihād.* Furthermore, *ijtihād* in this area does not entail an interpretation from the sources of the law, but aims instead, as does al-Ghazālī, to construct a set of arguments around legal concepts.

The central legal concept on which al-Ghazālī sets his arguments into motion is that of *farḍ* (religious obligation). He argues that al-Mustaẓhir fulfils the conditions (*sharāʾiṭ*) of the Imam, and hence he is God's *khalīfa* over mankind and obedience to him is a religious obligation (*farḍ*) incumbent on all mankind.[120] Recourse to the term *farḍ* enables al-Ghazālī to affirm the necessity of the Sunni caliph in every age, and to argue that contrary to those who uphold that there is nobody today who fulfils the requirements of the office, there will always be a qualified candidate in the Sunni community without whose existence the *sharīʿa* cannot be implemented.[121] In short, the caliph is an indispensable source of legitimacy, and all public appointments such as that of government officials and *qāḍīs* can only be valid if they issue forth from the caliph. However, it is interesting to note that al-Ghazālī does not specify how exactly al-Mustaẓhir qualifies for the *imāma,* except by putting forth the following syllogism:

Lā budda min imām fī kulli ʿaṣr
wa lā mutarashshiḥ li'l-imāma siwā-hu
fa-huwa al-imām al-ḥaqq idhan.

(There must be an Imam in every age,
but only he is qualified for the office;
therefore he is the rightful Imam.)[122]

This syllogism reinforces further the notion of *farḍ* in connection with the Sunni Imam, a notion that serves as a counterpoint to the absolutist claims of the Ismailis. Al-Ghazālī is here trying to construct an equally authoritative basis for al-Mustaẓhir, and his challenge lies in carving an alternative framework which is able to grant the same degree of centrality to al-Mustaẓhir as has been attributed to the Ismaili Imam. As such, emphasis on *farḍ* can be interpreted as a counterpoint to the Ismaili claim of *ʿiṣma* (infallibility) for their Imams.

The basis for this interpretation becomes more plausible when we take into account that the next legal concept on which al-Ghazālī develops his argument is *ijmāʿ*. Al-Ghazālī does not put forward a definition of *ijmāʿ*; yet it is evident from his use of it that, apart from acknowledging consensus as a source of law, for him it encapsulates the conception of a divinely guided community. It is a community whose judgement, following from the popular hadith, 'My community will never agree upon an error', is attributed with *ʿiṣma.*[123] For al-Ghazālī, *ijmāʿ* becomes a construct on which he develops a historical ideal of the community, an ideal which, among other things, affirms the necessity of electing an Imam to lead the community, so as to protect it from anarchy.[124] *Ikhtiyār* is the term used for 'election' and for al-Ghazālī it functions as an example of *ijmāʿ* in practice. The best historical example of this *ikhtiyār-ijmāʿ* nexus goes back to the earliest Companions who, in order to preserve the unity of the *umma* and the survival of Islam, acted speedily after the death of the Prophet to elect an Imam. Al-Ghazālī also points out that the election was of a single Imam and not a consultative council (*shūrā*).[125]

These, then, are the outlines of the alternative framework for al-Ghazālī's conception of the *imāma*, justifying itself by arguments both legal and historical – arguments which, furthermore, are also used polemically to demonstrate the invalidity of the Ismaili doctrine of *imāma*. In connection with the legal line of argument centred around the term *farḍ*, al-Ghazālī asserts that a fundamental precondition of the Imam is 'correctness of belief and soundness of religion' (*ṣiḥḥat al-ʿaqīda wa salāmat al-dīn*).[126]

Hence he argues that the already cited arguments for *takfīr* demonstrate clearly why the Ismaili Imam does not qualify. While in connection with the historical line of argument centred around the term *ijmāʿ*, al-Ghazālī points out that not only has the Ismaili conception of the Imam contravened *ijmāʿ* from the period of the earliest companions, but even at present the *ijmāʿ* (referring to its more literal connotation as a consensus of the majority) behind the Ismaili Imam is numerically negligible compared to the *ijmāʿ* of all 'the leaders and *ʿulamāʾ* of the age and by all the masses of men in farthest East and West' who recognize al-Mustaẓhir as their Imam.[127] These arguments are a clear illustration of the extent to which al-Ghazālī's *siyāsa sharʿiyya* formulation was interwoven with the broader polemical objectives of the text, so that al-Mustaẓhir's status had to be projected in terms which would in themselves serve as a sufficient counter-argument against the Bāṭiniyya.

It is this factor that can also help explain why al-Ghazālī makes no reference to the Saljuq sultan in this section; obviously al-Ghazālī was only too aware of the *de facto* power of his patrons, and hence his silence about the Saljuq sultan demands an explanation. Hitherto, two differing lines of explanation have been put forward. The first belongs to Lambton and Rosenthal which reads al-Ghazālī's silence as indicative of an early political idealism, and which very soon after was abandoned in favour of a posture of realpolitik, as is evident in *al-Iqtiṣād fī 'l-iʿtiqād*, where not only is the Saljuq sultan explicitly referred to but al-Ghazālī's thrust is to elaborate a theoretical basis for the sultan's relationship with the caliph.[128] The second explanation belongs to Hillenbrand who argues that al-Ghazālī was writing at a time of crisis and thus one has to read between the lines, leading her to conclude that though the Saljuq sultan is not explicitly mentioned, al-Ghazālī's message, albeit veiled, to the young al-Mustaẓhir was that he had no choice but to accept the continuing presence and power (*shawka*) of the Turks.[129] Hillenbrand's position is based on a much closer examination of the text and thus carries more weight than that of Lambton and Rosenthal. Even though I partly accept Hillenbrand's conclusions, some of the guiding assumptions of her approach, which incidentally are also shared by Lambton and Rosenthal, need to be re-examined and qualified further.

The problem here revolves around the use of the terms 'idealism' and 'realism' by these scholars when studying medieval Islamic political thought, especially their approach to *siyāsa sharʿiyya* texts. These terms embody assumptions about political life as it evolved in Europe; where, for example, idealism connotes a Platonic bias toward utopian thought, and realism connotes a Machiavellian persistence toward realpolitik. The conception of politics in *siyāsa sharʿiyya* texts is neither idealistic nor realistic in the above senses. Al-Ghazālī, for example, does not put forward a prescription for a perfect body politic, nor does he conceive of political authority or power solely in terms of expediency or pragmatism. For al-Ghazālī, and *siyāsa sharʿiyya* writers in general, the imperative is to maintain the *status quo*, which, because it was perceived to rest on *ijmāʿ*, had to be justified. As such, all *siyāsa sharʿiyya* texts are idealistic (if we are to use the term) in the sense that their authors were quite aware of their powerlessness to change political realities; hence these texts were primarily engaged in elaborating patterns of theoretical or *de jure* justification.[130] Concomitantly, if there is a strain of *realism* in these texts, it lies in their openness to adjust and refine their theoretical frameworks so as to keep pace with the unfolding of history.

Seen from this perspective, the best way to approach the *siyāsa sharʿiyya* section in the *K. al-Mustaẓhirī* is as a theoretical affirmation of the symbolic status of the caliph, al-Mustaẓhir. He becomes symbolic of the Sunni community and his status is placed in competition with that of the Ismaili Imam. Hence, it is highly probable that al-Ghazālī is silent about the Saljuqs because he wishes to affirm the theoretical autonomy of the caliph. Not because he wants to revive the *de facto* power which was once enjoyed by the Abbasid caliph, but merely because it would be polemically inexpedient to portray the status of the caliph as having been compromised by the presence of a Saljuq sultan. Nonetheless, al-Ghazālī could not completely turn a blind eye to the presence of the Saljuqs as such a denial would be tantamount to dishonesty, severely compromising al-Ghazālī's integrity and status as a member of the *ʿulamāʾ*. As a result, his formulation is not without its subtle manoeuvres and adjustments, allowing him, as Hillenbrand rightly observes, to strike a strategic balance between rationalizing the power and status of the Saljuqs (referred to as the Turks, *al-khalāʾiq al-turk*), while representing al-Mustaẓhir in terms sufficient enough to counter the sweeping claims made on behalf of the larger than life figure of the Fatimid/Ismaili/Taʿlīmiyya/Bāṭiniyya Imam.[131]

This pursuit of a strategic balance is what, for lack of a better phrase, could be referred to as the 'rhetoric of repair', of which al-Māwardī was perhaps the pioneering practitioner. Let us now turn our attention to specific examples of how al-Ghazālī worked out this strategic balance in the *K. al-Mustaẓhirī*.

After having introduced the idea of *ikhtiyār* (election), al-Ghazālī proceeds to defend its validity. This defence, apart from being framed in terms of a *kalām* style disputation, ends up refining and adjusting the definition of *ikhtiyār*. First, al-Ghazālī compares the designation of an Imam through *ikhtiyār* with that of the Ismaili claim of textual designation (*naṣṣ*). Recapitulating his earlier arguments that the texts in support of the Ismaili Imam are not *mutawātir* and are hence invalid, he affirms categorically that *ikhtiyār* is the only source (*maʾkhad*) for the Imamate.[131] Yet, soon after this affirmation, he begins to put forward some qualifications about the manner in which *ikhtiyār* is executed. He concedes that *ikhtiyār* does not rest on a universal nor actual *ijmāʿ* of the *ʿulamāʾ*, nor even of a specified number of people, but can in effect rest on the allegiance (*bayʿa*) of a single person:

> We choose to hold that one person can suffice if he is on the side of the majority (*al-jamāhīr*): his agreement is theirs.[133]

At this point, al-Ghazālī's pursuit of a strategic balance becomes ever more transparent, a pursuit which he elaborates into a theoretical framework, consisting of the following definitions and links. First, he upholds the centrality of *ijmāʿ* (consensus); second, he draws a link between *ijmāʿ* and *ikhtiyār* (election), whereby *ikhtiyār* becomes both an extension and an expression of *ijmāʿ*;

third, he goes on to make a further link between *ikhtiyār* and *bayʿa* (allegiance) of a single person, whereby the relationship between *bayʿa* and *ikhtiyār* is framed along lines similar to that between *ikhtiyār* and *ijmāʿ*. This entire framework reaches its climax when al-Ghazālī declares that the pre-condition for *bayʿa* is *shawka* (strength); in other words, the person making the oath of allegiance should be someone who is obeyed and possesses unsurpassed military strength, since his compliance represents the compliance of the masses.[134] This declaration functions as a climax in two important, yet different, respects: first, this is the furthest al-Ghazālī goes in implying both the presence of the Saljuq sultan and the extent to which the caliph is dependent on the one who is the possessor of *shawka*; second, al-Ghazālī turns full circle and asserts that, like *ijmāʿ*, the act of this *bayʿa* has to be divinely sanctioned:

> We have reduced the specification of the Imam to the choice of a single person; but really we have reduced it to God's choice and appointment (*ikhtiyār Allāh taʿālā wa nasbihi*). The real justification of the choice is that all follow and obey the Imam – a grace and gift of God, unattainable by any human contriving.[135]

Interestingly enough, soon after this passage al-Ghazālī goes on to praise al-Mustaẓhir, reiterating his status as the rightful Imam, as if to reassure his readers that, despite considerations of *shawka*, the authority of the caliph retains its autonomy and integrity. Thereafter, al-Ghazālī moves on to list the parameters of this authority. These parameters are described in terms of the necessary attributes or qualities (*ṣifāt*) which have to be embodied in the body and personality of the caliph. Examples of these attributes had become a standard feature of *siyāsa sharʿiyya*texts. Al-Ghazālī's list contains ten attributes, of which six are categorized as innate (*ṣifāt al-khilqī*) and four as acquired (*ṣifāt al-iktisāb*). The innate attributes function very much as pre-conditions and include: (i) *al-bulūgh* (maturity, attainment of puberty); (ii) *al-ʿaql* (intelligence); (iii) *al-ḥurriyya* (freedom); (iv) *al-dhukūr* (male sex); (v) *nasab Quraysh* (descent from

Quraysh clan of the Prophet); (vi) *salāma ḥāssat al-samʿ wa'l-baṣar* (soundness of hearing and sight).[136]

All the above attributes had been put forward by previous *siyāsa sharʿiyya* writers; al-Ghazālī is not adding anything new here. He also makes clear that it is the *ʿulamāʾ* who are responsible for enumerating these attributes.[137] This passing reference to the *ʿulamāʾ* serves as a hint of what will turn out to be a much more significant role that al-Ghazālī has in mind for the *ʿulamāʾ*. The elaboration of this role is connected with the remaining four acquired qualities of the Imam. These qualities function as ethical ideals. Their definition, as is the case with all ideals, is not a given but constitutes the subject matter of a theoretical inquiry. The acquired qualities include: (i) *al-najda* (bravery, military prowess); (ii) *al-kifāya* (political competence); (iii) *al-waraʿ* (piety); (iv) *al-ʿilm* (knowledge).

Al-Ghazālī provides a considerable amount of detail in defining these qualities, and from the approach and tone which is adopted it becomes clear that he is utilizing these qualities as vehicles for justifying the respective roles of the Saljuq establishment and also the *ʿulamāʾ* vis-à-vis Caliph al-Mustaẓhir.

Beginning with the quality of *najda*, al-Ghazālī once again returns to the issue of *shawka*, and quite unambiguously asserts:

> In this age of ours, from amongst the (various) kinds of human beings it is the Turks who possess *shawka*. Almighty God has given them the good fortune to befriend and love him (the caliph) to such an extent that they draw near to God by helping him (the caliph) and by suppressing the enemies of his state (*dawla*). They yield themselves to belief in his caliphate and *imāma*.[138]

Having acknowledged that the Turks are the possessors of *shawka*, al-Ghazālī goes on at length to explain that the Turks are obedient servants of the caliph and hence their *shawka* is ultimately to defend and uphold the authority of the caliph. As has been mentioned earlier, the self-styled role of the Saljuqs as guardians of the faith had been their long-standing political ambition; thus this measured defence of the Turks is but an exercise in rhetorical diplomacy on the part of al-Ghazālī. Overtones of an anti-Bāṭiniyya polemic can also be heard when al-Ghazālī praises the Turks as those who the caliph can depend on to wage a *jihād* against the infidels.[139]

Turning his attention to the quality of *kifāya* (political competence), al-Ghazālī begins by describing the current period as being one of crisis, applying to it the Qur'anic term *fatra* (effacement of the signs of religion).[140] Though he does not spell out the causes or the precise nature of this crisis, it is in all likelihood a reference to either the infiltration of the Bāṭiniyya or to the as yet unresolved Saljuq civil war, or perhaps to the combined impact of both these factors. Be that as it may, al-Ghazālī oscillates between praising al-Mustaẓhir's astuteness and powers of discrimination to bring about order and stability, while also stressing that the caliph will have to ensure that he is surrounded by competent advisers – men of insight and experience – placing special emphasis on the appointment of a strong *wazīr*.[141] At the end of this section, we are left unsure as to where exactly lies the locus of *kifāya*: is it pre-eminently subsumed in the office and figure of the caliph, or does it arise out of the collaborative relationship between the caliph and his court? In his effort to bolster the status of the caliph, al-Ghazālī ends up transposing the model of the then powerful Saljuq court (inclusive of the *wizāra*) onto the caliphate. This transposition is again intended more as a rhetorical strategy, undertaken not to fulfil any concrete political objectives, but a way of dignifying the perceived authority of the caliphate.

The third quality of *wara*ʿ (piety) is discussed in terms which are at once predictable and very general. Cultivation of piety becomes incumbent upon the caliph, and emphasis is placed on how this responsibility falls squarely on the caliph himself, and that no manner of outside agency can help him in this matter.[142] Much of the material here is couched in the tone of exhortation, and it constitutes a preliminary sketch of what will be covered in much greater detail when he takes up the 'mirrors for princes' genre in Chapter 10.

Finally, with the quality of *ʿilm* (knowledge) al-Ghazālī touches on issues most pertinent to himself, namely, the nature of the caliph's relationship to the *ʿulamāʾ*, and hence also the status of the *ʿulamāʾ* within a conception of an Islamic body politic. Right at the outset, al-Ghazālī makes clear that the specific connotation carried by the term *ʿilm* is here connected with a knowledge of the law, further specifying it as the knowledge which enables one to attain 'the rank of *ijtihād* and [hence] give a *fatwā* in the science of the law (*ʿulūm al-sharʿ*)'.[143] Moreover, the *ʿulamāʾ* have made the possession of this knowledge a condition for the Imam. Yet he does not clearly explain why this knowledge constitutes an indispensable condition, apart from asserting that to deny this would constitute a departure from the opinions of past *ʿulamāʾ*.[144] Al-Ghazālī's challenge is to justify how al-Mustaẓhir, whom he acknowledges as being not yet in possession of the requisite level of legal knowledge, can nonetheless exercise his authority as caliph. He argues that just as the caliph depends on competent advisers in matters of *kifāya*, similarly he can consult and depend on the *ʿulamāʾ* on matters of *ʿilm*. After re-affirming al-Mustaẓhir's right to the caliphate, al-Ghazālī goes so far as to articulate the caliph's dependence on the *ʿulamāʾ* in terms of the following two conditions:

> One is that he not settle any problem except after exploiting the talents of the *ʿulamāʾ* and seeking their help, and when in doubt choose to follow the best and most learned – the City of Peace [Baghdad] will rarely be without such men. The second is that he seek to acquire knowledge and gain rank of independence in the science of the law – for God has enjoined the acquisition of knowledge. He is young enough to do that in a short time.[145]

The above passage, concluding, as it does, the *siyāsa sharʿiyya* section, amounts ingeniously to an exercise in self-advertisement, whereby the centrality of not only the *ʿulamāʾ* but of his own position is alluded to, as is implicit in the very fact that he can be bold enough to set conditions for al-Mustaẓhir. As such, al-Ghazālī ensures that the *ʿulamāʾ* become key mediating players in matters of both authority and power. There is a tone of urgency here because al-Ghazālī is only too aware of the precarious and ever shifting balance through which the agencies of authority and power were then sustaining themselves.

A question of balance emerges once again in Chapter 10, the finale to the text. But balance here is of a different kind altogether, concerning itself with the duties (*waẓā'if*) of *al-ʿilmiyya* (knowledge) and *al-ʿamaliyya* (action/deeds). They constitute the two poles around which al-Ghazālī addresses his counsels to Caliph al-Mustaẓhir.[146] These counsels are structured around a set of ethical ideals and function symbolically as mirrors by which the caliph can continually observe and improve himself. In practical terms this genre served as a construct for narcissism, whereby the respective ethical ideals were already assumed to be embodied in whoever was the addressee of these counsels; hence the tone of exhortation common to this genre functioned as a disguise for what was in effect a tribute confirming the 'worthiness' (*istiḥqāq*) of the candidate. That the candidate here is al-Mustaẓhir follows inevitably from al-Ghazālī's claim that the caliph had commissioned him to write this text – further personifying the *Faḍā'il al-mustaẓhiriyya.*

However, such glowing praise of al-Mustaẓhir would not have been completely devoid of political significance, whether intended or not by al-Ghazālī. Especially when one takes into consideration that al-Ghazālī had later in his life dedicated a text of the same genre, entitled *Naṣīḥat al-mulūk*, to the Saljuq Sultan Sanjar.[147] The point here is that this genre had its own political prestige, and hence what needs to be ascertained is the exact nature of the prestige being accorded to al-Mustaẓhir. We will return to this question later on, but first let us put forward some general observations about the contents of this chapter.

Perhaps the most striking feature is that the entire section, as befitting the genre, is packed with metaphors and allegories. The most recurrent image used is that of the body: recognizing the ephemerality of the body in contrast to the afterlife of the soul; the need to govern the body and its passions; and just as the body requires nourishment so does the soul.[148] These so-called leitmotifs and the vocabulary in which they are conveyed carry obvious Sufi provenance. Al-Ghazālī's Sufism lies beyond the scope of this study, but the material here is relevant for understanding the formative traces of his Sufi inclinations. Even when discussing themes such as justice and the *sharīʿa* in connection to *al-ʿamaliyya* of the caliph, al-Ghazālī's style is still metaphorical, though the discussion is always supported by copious references to the Qurʾan and hadith. It is in the context of *al-ʿamaliyya* (deeds), and not *al-ʿilmiyya* (knowledge), that al-Ghazālī once again points out the necessity for the caliph to consult the *ʿulamāʾ*.[149]

As much as this section is also about governance, its overall effect is to impart a highly abstract conception of moral governance, where the practical realities of the body politic carry no significance – what matters are the ideals themselves, ideals which are disembodied from the pre-occupations of any systematic discipline, be it of law or theology. Carole Hillenbrand, when referring to al-Ghazālī's subsequently written 'mirrors for princes' texts, reads them as indicative of his growing disillusionment with the political systems of his time, and hence his emphasis on 'personal piety and the transitory nature of this world'.[150] That being the case, how does one explain the juxtaposition in the *K. al-Mustaẓhirī* of two differing genres of political thought: a highly intricate *siyāsa sharʿiyya* section followed immediately by a 'mirror for princes'? I do not believe that in this case the explanation of an overall disillusionment can hold water, nor does Hillenbrand offer this, or indeed any other interpretation with regard to the *K. al-Mustaẓhirī*, as if the issue were of no significance. I do not think this juxtaposition can altogether be ignored, although the conclusions to be drawn at present can be no more than conjectural or speculative.

Taken together, both these chapters have the cumulative effect of associating the personality of al-Mustaẓhir with more than just symbolic importance. The conspicuous references made to al-Mustaẓhir throughout the text elevate him to a very distinguished status, brimming with a tangible sense of expectation and pride. All of this cannot be explained merely in terms of polemical strategy, such that this representation of al-Mustaẓhir is seen solely as a counterpoint to the Ismaili Imam. In addition, there is a soft, yet pervasive, ethos of revivalism in al-Ghazālī's treatment of the caliphate in the *K. al-Mustaẓhirī*. Again, it should be borne in mind that this posture of al-Ghazālī sought to ameliorate not so much the actual status of the caliph but his perceived status.

Two distinct, yet somewhat interdependent, lines of explanation could serve as additional background factors for this revivalist posture. First, it could be argued that al-Ghazālī had become convinced that not only the person of the caliph but the office itself was under serious threat of dissolution. Signs of this had become manifest in the policies of the Saljuq sultan, Malik Shāh and equally also through the activities of the *wazīr* Niẓām al-Mulk. Wael B. Hallaq has argued that the potential weight of Niẓām al-Mulk's personality is intimated in al-Juwaynī's *siyāsa sharʿiyya* treatise entitled *Ghiyāth al-umam*,[151] where, according to Hallaq, al-Juwaynī, apart from questioning the necessity of a caliph who is militarily and politically powerless, was in effect inviting Niẓām al-Mulk to occupy the office of caliph. According to al-Juwaynī, Niẓām al-Mulk was eligible because it was he, and not the caliph, who was in possession of what to al-Juwaynī were the two central qualifications for the office: *istiqlāl* (political independence) and *kifāya* (political competence).[152] This being the case, al-Ghazālī's posture in the *K. al-Mustaẓhirī* and subsequently can be seen as a reaction to this sort of thinking, a reaction which was motivated by the conviction that the perceived authority and necessity of the caliphate was central to the unity and stability of the Muslim community.

A second line of explanation grows out of this same conviction, but focuses on the nature of the *ʿulamā*'s dependence on the caliph. As has been made obvious in this study, al-Ghazālī perceived the *ʿulamāʾ* as deriving their legitimacy from the caliphate. Hence any effort to enhance the status of al-Mustaẓhir would concomitantly have fortified the role and place of the *ʿulamāʾ*. The probability of this revivalist posture is made all the more plausible if we take into account the fact of the Saljuq civil war. The war provided al-Ghazālī the space for such a posture, without his running the risk of offending the Saljuq establishment, which was then far too consumed with other issues to take notice of the *K. al-Mustaẓhirī*.

Seen from this perspective, both Chapters 9 and 10 are imbued with the spirit of rehabilitating the caliphate, a process of rehabilitation which, nonetheless, was only too conscious of the irreversible constraints that would continue to impinge on the actual status of the caliph. The juxtaposition of these two chapters can, hence, be seen as part of a complementary strategy through which al-Ghazālī endeavoured to rehabilitate the Sunni caliphate to the furthest extent possible.

CHAPTER THREE

Towards a Re-reading of the *Kitāb al-Mustaẓhirī*

The historical study of ideas is concerned primarily with questions of significance and influence. One of the primary aims of this study has been to recover the historical significance and influence of the *K. al-Mustaẓhirī*. It is a fascinating and complex text; its ideas capture not only the great questions of the age in which it was written, but also carry an uncanny relevance for the intellectual predicaments facing Muslims in the contemporary world. Building on the contextual (historical) map that was drawn out in Chapter One of this book, and on the structure of the text that was laid bare in Chapter Two, this chapter will now analyse more broadly the ideas contained in al-Ghazālī's text. This analysis will take the form of re-reading the work, with a view to exploring the ways in which its arguments and themes were and continue to be emblematic of key concerns in the history of Muslim thought.

Every re-reading entails the act of manipulation which consists of applying a set of perspectives from the present onto a text written in the past. Hence, a re-reading is conditioned by the distance in time between the composition of a text and when the re-reading is undertaken; the greater the distance, the more pervasive is the manipulation. With the *K. al-Mustaẓhirī* the distance is that which separates the medieval from the modern, and this study has been extremely conscious of that distance. The medieval character of the text has so far been the object of a reconstruction and a translation in this study: a reconstruction of the environment in which al-Ghazālī wrote; and a translation, in the broadest sense of the word, of the terms and arguments contained in it. The insights derived from this reconstruction and translation will now be used for undertaking a critical analysis of the text.

The *K. al-Mustaẓhirī* is a dense and many-sided text, containing diverse styles of argumentation and presentation, each of which addresses a distinct set of conceptual concerns. For the purposes of our re-reading, we will classify these conceptual concerns as belonging to the categories of orthodoxy, reason and authority. Al-Ghazālī, it will be argued, struggled with problems and questions connected to each of these three categories, which serve as themes (or *topoi*) for al-Ghazālī's central arguments in this work. They are not al-Ghazālī's categories, but a set of perspectives projected (manipulated, if you will) onto the text. Yet, hopefully, the ensuing analysis will demonstrate their cogency for appreciating its intellectual and historical significance.

Orthodoxy: A Problem of Interpretation

That the use of the term 'orthodoxy' is highly problematic when applied to Islam has been commented on by several scholars, of whom Goldziher was the most perceptive in pointing out that:

> The dogma of Islam cannot be compared with the same constituent part of the religion of any of the Christian churches. There are no councils and synods which, after vigorous debate, can establish the formulae that must stand henceforth as the symbol of the true faith. There is no ecclesiastical function which represents the criterion of orthodoxy; there is no exegesis exclusively authorized by the sacred texts on which the doctrinal method and substance of the church rests. Consensus [*ijmāʿ*], the highest authority in all questions of religious theory and practice, is an expandable spring, [and thus it is] difficult to reach agreement

on what should pass unquestionably for consensus. What one party regards as such, another will reject.[1]

Yet despite the lack of an official, centralized authority, as in Christianity, to enforce an orthodoxy, the history of Islamic law and theology bears witness to a perennial desire to claim and argue for an orthodoxy. The *K. al-Mustaẓhirī* is a prime example of this desire, where, apart from harnessing it to arguments derived from *adab al-firaq*, *kalām*, *fiqh* and *uṣūl al-fiqh* (each a potential crucible for orthodoxy), al-Ghazālī employs the term *takfīr* to map out the boundaries of an orthodox position. A distinction needs therefore to be made between the practical authoritativeness as opposed to the theoretical expressions of orthodoxy in Islam. Although Goldziher was right in his assertion that the history of Islam has been devoid of an institutionalized agency or mouthpiece for orthodoxy, nevertheless the history of Sunni Islam is replete with examples of political forces and actors seeking to assert an orthodoxy. A case in point is the establishment of the Niẓāmiyya college in Baghdad where, arguably, al-Ghazālī wrote the *K. al-Mustaẓhirī*. This brings to the foreground another distinction, that between the institutionalized manifestation as opposed to the ideological pursuit of orthodoxy in Islamic history.

The polemical orientation of the *K. al-Mustaẓhirī* is at once theoretical and ideological, a conjunction which is most articulately expressed in al-Ghazālī's *fatwā* of unbelief (*takfīr*). At the theoretical level, al-Ghazālī laboured to justify the legal basis and implications of this *fatwā*; at the ideological level, the *fatwā* becomes an instrument of exclusion and violence. On both levels, the posture is predominantly reactive; hence orthodoxy is defined with reference to what lies outside it rather than to what it stands for *per se*. This is clearly borne out by the fact that there is no adequate equivalent for the term 'orthodoxy' in Arabic. For al-Ghazālī, the conception of a normative centre is perhaps best conveyed by the phrase: *ahl al-sunna wa'l-jamā'a* (people of the prophetic tradition and of the community/consensus).[2] This expression, apart from being a descriptive label, is itself open to varied definitions, and in fact accommodates a degree of dissent and diversity as incorporated through the principle of *ikhtilāf*– allowing different schools of Sunni law to co-exist on equal terms with each other.

By resorting to the *fatwā* of *takfīr*, al-Ghazālī was trying to establish the limits of tolerable dissent. As mentioned earlier, of all the accusations levelled against the Ismailis/Bāṭiniyya, it is only on one specific issue that he places them in the position of having transgressed the limits of tolerable dissent, namely, their interpretation of what is meant by Resurrection (*qiyāma*) in the Qur'an. Hence, al-Ghazālī's *fatwā* amounts to a legal ruling on a point of doctrine, and in this sense his presumed domain of orthodoxy rests on both a legal and theological interpretation – that is, on an interdependence between law and theology.

Al-Ghazālī was writing at a time when the disciplines of law and theology were still very much in the throes of defining their respective boundaries in relation to each other, let alone the basis of their interdependence. George Makdisi's research has been seminal in re-tracing the complex historical relationship between law and theology in medieval Islam, drawing attention to the evolution of distinctions that emerged between, for example, *fiqh* and *uṣūl al-fiqh* or between *kalām* and *uṣūl al-dīn*, and more importantly, the degrees of co-operation with which all these disciplines interrelated.[3] Examples of all these evolving distinctions are contained in the *K. al-Mustaẓhirī*, and one of the central concerns of the text has been to demonstrate the instrumental interdependence of law and theology in constructing a conception of orthodoxy in Islam.

This conception is highly reified; it is not so much a textual prescription but an attitude of orthodoxy. At the very core of this attitude is the assumption that the disciplines of law and theology are systems of interpretation, and hence orthodoxy is ultimately not a given postulate but represents a problem of interpretation.[4] The object of interpretation is the Qur'an, be it to discover and implement God's law or to understand the nature of God and of His commandments. In the *K. al-Mustaẓhirī*, law and theology are used as tools applied systematically with the purpose of refuting the Bāṭiniyya and their interpretations, and it is in the very application of these tools that an attitude, not a definition, of orthodoxy is vindicated. Al-Ghazālī would not have claimed as much – for to declare that the issue of orthodoxy revolved solely around questions of interpretation would have been tantamount to making the truth seem relative. For al-Ghazālī there existed absolute religious truths, yet truths that one had to strive towards, and law and theology as systems of interpretation were but paths toward, and not constructions of, these absolute truths. Interpretation, be it through *ijtihād* or *ta'wīl*, is dedicated to discovering (or uncovering) what God has already revealed to mankind.

Leaving aside the issue of interpretation, the most tangible way in which the *K. al-Mustaẓhirī* expressed an attitude of orthodoxy is through the framework of moral opposition, whereby the Bāṭiniyya are portrayed in categories of moral deviance in complete opposition to the presumed moral centre from which al-Ghazālī is writing. There is no better example of this than the very title of the text: *Faḍā'iḥ al-Bāṭiniyya wa faḍā'il al-Mustaẓhiriyya* (The Infamies of the Bāṭiniyya and the Virtues of the Mustaẓhiriyya). It is this charged tone of moral polemic that enables al-Ghazālī to project a confident affirmation of orthodoxy without ever openly conceding that it is rooted in an engaged process of legal and theological interpretation.

Reason: Subjectivity versus Objectivity

An enquiry into the definition and role of reason features quite prominently in the *K. al-Mustaẓhirī*. This enquiry is in the first instance fuelled by his refutation of the *ta'līm* doctrine. However there is another more pervasive, yet subtle, dimension which gives rise to this enquiry, namely, his attempt to carve out a place for reason in Sunni law and theology. Al-Ghazālī's attempt can be best characterized as a process of integration, avoiding the excesses, hitherto expressed in Islamic history, of a literalist rejection of, or a philosophical subservience to, reason. As mentioned earlier, the *K. al-Mustaẓhirī* serves as the earliest record of al-

Ghazālī's use of the syllogism in his writings, and in relation to which he uses the term *naẓar* for reason. Whether, or to what extent this term was a representative designation for reason in *uṣūl al-fiqh* and *kalām* texts up until the time of al-Ghazālī, is a question that has yet to be adequately explored by scholars. Wael B. Hallaq's writings on legal theory and Richard M. Frank's on *kalām* methodology have been breaking new ground in this direction.[5]

The focus here will be limited to an examination of the objectives underlying al-Ghazālī's need to integrate reason. This integration is, broadly speaking, marked by two objectives: practical and theoretical. At the practical level, al-Ghazālī set out to defend reason against what he perceived to be the anti-rationalist perspective of the *taʿlīm* doctrine, a perspective which was not a simple rejection of reason but an argument claiming that human reason is fallible and hence there is a necessity for an infallible teacher, such as the Ismaili Imam, to guide mankind. Correspondingly, the Ismailis argued, those without access to this *taʿlīm* dispensed by the infallible Imam, as is the case of the Sunni community, will continue to be misguided by their inescapable dependence on fallible conjecture (*ẓann*) and speculation derived from human reasoning.

Al-Ghazālī knew only too well the implications of this doctrine, which amounted to an indictment of the entire framework of Sunni thought, dependent as it is on the use of human reason in the formulation and application of its law and theology. Hence the challenge confronting al-Ghazālī was to both refute the perspective of the *taʿlīm* doctrine while concomitantly defending the place of reason in Sunni thought. This challenge was a practical imperative in so far as it sought to defuse the politico-ideological threat of the Bāṭiniyya and fortify the authority and integrity of his own position as a member of the Sunni *ʿulamāʾ* – or more specifically as a Shāfiʿī-Ashʿarī writer. On the issue of the *taʿlīm* doctrine, al-Ghazālī's refutation can be summed up by the argument that as much as the *taʿlīm* doctrine would want to claim the necessity of an infallible teacher and the invalidation of human reasoning, it is a claim that is supported by means of a rational argument, and hence fully dependent on the very grounds of human reasoning which the doctrine purports to be fallible. Thus he defines this doctrine as being a case of circularity, of trying to invalidate reason through the use of reason.

However, this refutation still leaves unanswered the general question whether human reasoning *per se* is fallible or infallible. Al-Ghazālī does not confront this question head on, but arrives at a response which begins as part of his defence of the use of reason in Sunni law and theology. He affirms the existence of an infallible teacher who, though, is the Prophet alone, and who had himself sanctioned the use of individual reasoning (*ijtihād al-ra'y*). Al-Ghazālī does not leave it at that but took it upon himself to define the nature, scope and role of this sanctioned reason, setting into motion an elaborate theoretical analysis of reason. Apart from defining the role of reason in relation to different types of knowledge – revelational, intellectual and juridical – he puts forward a conception of reason as being a method, and this method was Aristotelian logic (a concatenation of premises and proofs), which if used correctly can be a reliable guide in the pursuit of knowledge. It is this method which al-Ghazālī endeavoured systematically to integrate into the disciplines of law and theology.

An extremely perspicacious interpretation of the *K. al-Mustaẓhirī's* integrationist agenda was put forward by Josef van Ess in the article 'Scepticism in Islamic Religious Thought', where he argues that al-Ghazālī turned to the syllogism as a means of introducing a criterion of objectivity into the arguments and interpretations put forward by the disciplines of law and theology. According to van Ess, al-Ghazālī's primary aim was to counter the unbridled subjectivity implied in arguments such as that of the *taʿlīm* doctrine, articulating, as it did, a philosophical scepticism to be resolved only by recourse to a locus of authority outside and beyond human reasoning – a 'scepticism for belief's sake'.[6] As for the significance of al-Ghazālī's pursuit of objectivity through the syllogism, van Ess makes the following perceptive observations:

> It is al-Ghazālī who, for the first time, imperatively stressed the epistemological problem: nobody needs *taʿlīm*, instruction by an Imam, because speculation can be safely conducted to an undoubtable result. One must only use an infallible method, and this infallible method is Aristotelian logic. It was due to the Bāṭinite attack – due to scepticism – that the *mutakallimūn* understood that one does not only need results but also the method to defend them; the best truth loses much of its value when it is not imperative by its own power. We must, however, not overlook one fact: the victory of syllogism was, too, the victory of mental rigidity; syllogism was good for the administration of spiritual wealth, but it was of nearly no use for the investment of this wealth into new projects. Those who were not gifted for speculation felt themselves more removed than before; they chose the only outlet they could find, the way into Sufism. It was al-Ghazālī himself who had opened them this door.[7]

Authority: Spiritual versus Temporal

It is perhaps too obvious to even need stating that the *K. al-Mustaẓhirī* addresses itself to issues of authority. Indeed these issues pervade the entire text. Yet what is equally obvious and even striking is that, despite the pervasiveness of these issues, the conception of authority in this text does not reduce itself to any single clear definition or term, but is rather layered with such a varied set of connotations and implications that the very usefulness of applying the concept of authority becomes an analytical problem in and of itself. This problem is not peculiar to this text, nor even to al-Ghazālī's thought, but is a wider problem associated with the study of Islam, be it as a religion or a civilization.

The roots of the problem lie both outside and within the history of Islam. Coming from the outside, it presents itself as a terminological issue, while from within it arises out of the very circumstances of historical evolution. The terminological issue emerges out of the European encounter with the Muslim world, and in particular the attendant rise of Oriental studies whereby

European scholars studying Islamic history inevitably transposed terminological categories of European history, such as *church* and *state* or *religious* and *secular*, onto the history of Islam.[8] In an attempt to redress the obvious shortcomings of this approach, orientalist scholarship was confronted with two choices: either to abandon completely any sort of transposition of concepts and terms and hence emphasize the historical uniqueness (or complete otherness) of Islam, leading to an elaboration of a separate terminology altogether; or to become more conscious of, yet not reject, the limitations of projecting European categories of authority onto Islam, and also striving constantly to adjust these categories so as to reflect fully both the comparative uniqueness and similarity of Muslim history vis-à-vis the history of Europe. Both these alternatives have a tendency to overlook the dynamic historical evolution of Islam, so that, for example, there is not one conception but rather several conceptions of authority, some of which are unique to Islam and others are not. The issue at stake here is not merely one of historical periodization, but of an historical consciousness that is continually being shaped by the challenges and questions around the issue of authority.[9]

Drawing on categories developed by Max Weber, authority in Islam can be analysed in terms of a framework structured around two broad temporal phases: the emergence and expressions of authority during the lifetime of the Prophet Muḥammad, followed by the emergence of post-Prophetic articulation and struggle between different conceptions of authority.[10] This framework brings to light the varied complexities confronting Muslims themselves when engaging with issues of authority, of which the central predicament is that all succeeding generations of Muslims after the death of the Prophet have continuously struggled to maintain a link with the charismatic authority and example of the Prophet. The Prophet's mission and personality is the locus of charisma which is reified into a model of authority directly addressing the Muslim community. Different responses to this authority crystallized over time: for example, the *ahl al-sunna* sought to institutionalize this charismatic authority, articulating it through the institution of the *khilāfa* and the disciplines of law and theology; while the Shiʿa sought to perpetuate this charismatic authority through the doctrine of *imāma*. Both these responses represent a type of transposition, where the Prophetic model is the originating source which is transposed and kept alive with the march of post-Prophetic history. The model of the Prophet's authority is total, an indivisible expression of the spiritual and temporal, while the expressions of authority in the post-Prophetic period have to accept to varying degrees the distinctions between the spiritual and temporal, which emerge through the need to either rationalize or negotiate a link between different forms of institutionalized authority.

All the aforementioned observations have a bearing on how to examine the issues of authority articulated in the *K. al-Mustaẓhirī*. It represents a snapshot of a significant moment in the post-Prophetic engagement with the concept of authority. Three issues stand out in particular: the status of the caliph; the identity of the *ʿulamāʾ*; and the commitments of al-Ghazālī's religious conscience. Each issue articulates a relationship to authority in medieval Islam, and in each case a relationship which, for al-Ghazālī, presents itself as a problem calling for resolution and clarification.

Much has already been said about al-Ghazālī's preoccupation with the caliphate, encompassing the following key factors: the vulnerability of Caliph al-Mustaẓhir in his relationship with the Saljuqs; the impact of the Ismaili Imam's ideological challenge; and the motives underlying al-Ghazālī's proto-caliphal stand in the *K. al-Mustaẓhirī*. However, there is one significant aspect that has not yet been touched upon and that is al-Ghazālī's use of the terms *al-dīn* and *al-dunyā* to designate different spheres of the caliph's authority. This distinction is referred to in various passages throughout the text, and it is perhaps the closest equivalent we have to the division between spiritual (*dīn*) and temporal (*dunyā*) authority.[11] In subsequent texts al-Ghazālī develops and applies this distinction in a far more structured manner than is the case in the *K. al-Mustaẓhirī*.[12] Nevertheless, his embryonic usage of these terms in this work encapsulates quite clearly the situation confronting the status of the Sunni caliph. On the one hand, this distinction points to the potential divisions of authority between the caliph and the Saljuq sultan, whereby the caliph, on the basis of his religious authority, delegates to the sultan jurisdiction over temporal affairs. On the other hand, this distinction was used as a construct to emphasize how the caliph was, indeed, the locus of authority in both these spheres, so as to challenge the allegedly comprehensive status (in both spheres) of the Ismaili Imam. Thus it is that al-Ghazālī has to negotiate the authority of Caliph al-Mustaẓhir between the implications of both these positions. In relation to the Saljuq sultan, the caliph's status is inevitably diluted; in relation to the Ismaili Imam, the incompatibility between the Sunni and Shiʿa conceptions of *imāma* still had to be maintained.

The theme of authority emerges somewhat more indirectly with respect to the identity of the *ʿulamāʾ*. Though the *K. al-Mustaẓhirī* addresses the challenges and questions in this area, yet al-Ghazālī addresses them rather obliquely. It is through the intellectual approach and style of the text that he appears subtly to be making claims on behalf of the *ʿulamāʾ*. Before entering the text, it would be appropriate to lay out the general parameters within which the identity of *ʿulamāʾ* is, in the first place, perceived to be problematic. To begin with, the historical emergence of the *ʿulamāʾ* was an almost organic extension of the Muslim community itself; hence its role and function, especially as a distinct corporate body within the community, was not only subject to an amorphous evolution but lacked a clear cut, practical terms of reference. The term *ʿulamāʾ* was a highly flexible term applicable to a diverse range of individuals, performing religious, legal, educational and even political functions. Aziz Al-Azmeh in his highly suggestive book, *Arabic Thought and Islamic Societies*, refers to the *ʿulamāʾ* as an 'imaginary class' in medieval Islam, adding very aptly: 'The ideological collectivity *ʿulamāʾ* as well as the concept of *ʿulamāʾ*, are equally utopian collectivities and utopian concepts'.[13]

Following from this, the other important consideration relates to the fact which Al-Azmeh points out: 'This group carried knowledge, and its members were the producers, preservers and distributors of knowledge'.[14] The question that arises here is what sort of knowledge is carried by the *ʿulamāʾ*; put differently, to what processes of learning and teaching did the *ʿulamāʾ* dedicate themselves? As can be gathered from the foregoing observations, the so-called problematic identity of the *ʿulamāʾ* is connected very much with how we today make sense of the ways and means by which the *ʿulamāʾ* cultivated and expressed themselves in medieval Islam.

That the *K. al-Mustaẓhirī* throws up these issues is quite obvious, judging solely from the fact that al-Ghazālī refers consciously to himself as a member of the *ʿulamāʾ*, and as we know he was not just an ordinary member but occupied the highest official post at the Niẓāmiyya college in Baghdad. In fact, as mentioned earlier, the very emergence of the Niẓāmiyya network served as an instrument in forging an identity and a role for the *ʿulamāʾ*. The Niẓāmiyya as an institution was responsible for promoting an identity rooted in a Shāfiʿī-Ashʿarī justification of the *ʿulamāʾ* as embodying an extension of the caliph's authority, enabling them to assert their role as interpreters and guardians of the law – a role to which al-Ghazālī makes several references throughout the text.[15] The *K. al-Mustaẓhirī* is an example of how he articulates himself in the role of interpreter and guardian of the law, even though the text embraces so much more than just the law. Al-Ghazālī appears to imply that though the forte of the *ʿulamāʾ* lay in their knowledge of the law, yet they are also to be seen as intellectuals, in the broadest sense of the term, whose curiosity and expertise should not only be limited to the religious or legal sciences (*al-ʿulūm al-dīniyya/al-sharʿiyya*), but also encompass the rational sciences (*al-ʿulūm al-ʿaqliyya*). He employs this distinction in order to separate the knowledge of the law from all other classes of knowledge, a distinction, which, once again, is applied less systematically in the *K. al-Mustaẓhirī* than in his subsequent writings, especially the *Iḥyāʾ ʿulūm al-dīn*.[16]

The remarkable range of approaches and styles in the *K. al-Mustaẓhirī* is a testimony to al-Ghazālī's dexterity in embracing a variety of disciplines, limited not only to the legal. Here and elsewhere, he writes with an acute self-awareness of the formal categories and limitations within differing disciplines or classes of knowledge. No place is this better demonstrated then in *al-Munqidh min al-ḍalāl*, where al-Ghazālī defines the approach of the Mutakallimūn, Bāṭiniyya (al-Taʿlīmiyya), Falāsifa and Sufis, and examines their ideas as being what we would today call 'modes of discourse'. Al-Ghazālī subjects the ideas of each discipline to a form of rational criticism, so as to evaluate their respective depth and limitations.[17] Even though the discipline of law as such is not treated as a discourse in *al-Munqidh*, al-Ghazālī's *uṣūl al-fiqh* text, *al-Mustaṣfā min ʿilm al-uṣūl*, approaches the law very much as a discourse whose intellectual authority is open to rationalization.[18]

The combination of al-Ghazālī's diverse intellectual inclinations and, moreover, his critical self-awareness of this diversity adds another question to the whole issue connected with the identity of the *ʿulamāʾ* – namely, that if knowledge *per se* served as a source of authority, what then was the depth and scope of knowledge from which the *ʿulamāʾ* could and perhaps should derive their identity? This question lies at the heart of several of al-Ghazālī's major texts, and the *K. al-Mustaẓhirī* is one of them. He returned to this issue time and again with an almost inexhaustible curiosity, ever elaborating different perspectives throughout his life.

Al-Ghazālī displayed an equally restless curiosity in his confrontation with the Ismailis, a confrontation which, according to Marshall G.S. Hodgson, 'is too intimate, and is taken up in diverse forms too repeatedly, to be accounted for in a purely external way. He [al-Ghazālī] refuted the Ismailis over and over, I think, because he found something in their position to be persuasive.'[19] Admittedly, an enquiry into what may constitute the 'internal' factors or explanations for al-Ghazālī's confrontation is a highly tenuous undertaking. Without going so far as to presume that we can fully understand the workings of his mind, we shall here, nevertheless, endeavour to explore the plausibility of how and in what senses al-Ghazālī found the doctrines of the so-called Bāṭiniyya 'persuasive'.

As mentioned earlier, the Bāṭiniyya were not only a political threat, they also constituted an intellectual challenge to Sunni Islam. Intellectually, the position of the Ismailis which al-Ghazālī challenged was that formulated by Ḥasan-i Ṣabbāḥ in his doctrine of *taʿlīm.* According to al-Shahrastānī's version of this doctrine, in every age, religious authority resides in, and is disseminated by, one uniquely qualified teacher whose legitimacy demands no extrinsic proof other than the need of mankind for such a teacher. Hence every individual has to seek out and commit himself unconditionally to this teacher. The complete autonomy of the teacher implies that the role of individual reasoning in pursuing the truth is, of necessity, subordinated (or, as al-Ghazālī would have it, invalidated) to the authority of this teacher. Al-Ghazālī's refutation of this position involves not a repudiation of such a teacher but re-definition of the teacher as the Prophet alone, and a re-affirmation of the role of reason as being both sanctioned by the Prophet and as a necessary tool (yet neutral and limited by the authority of revelation) in pursuing the Truth.

Marshall Hodgson and W. Montgomery Watt have argued that al-Ghazālī did not so much reject the premises of the *taʿlīm* doctrine but adapted them to the needs and situation of the Sunni community.[20] The framework of this adaptation is latent in the *K. al-Mustaẓhirī*, though it is elaborated more comprehensively in *al-Qiṣṭās al-mustaqīm* and the *Munqidh*, and can be summarized thus: whereas the *taʿlīm* doctrine places sole emphasis on the authority of a living teacher, al-Ghazālī sought to connect the Prophet's *taʿlīm* with that of a living, historical community, so that the cumulative experience of the Sunni community becomes the repository and continuing guarantor of truth for every individual believer. A precarious balancing act can be read into what, in effect, amounts to al-Ghazālī's *re-reading* of the *taʿlīm* doctrine. It represents a balancing act between individualistic as opposed to communalistic conceptions of religious authority. For al-Ghazālī, the *taʿlīm* doctrine was, apart from its self-contradictory position on reason, also excessively individualistic. It assumes that every individual could by himself realize the necessity for seeking guidance from an authoritative teacher, and hence completely overlooks the role of the community in nurturing and sustaining the authority of any teacher – and so it is that al-Ghazālī affirms the necessity of both a teacher and a community. In the *K. al-Mustaẓhirī*, the necessity of the community is articulated in terms of al-Ghazālī's recurrent emphasis on the centrality of the law as the *raison d'être* of the Muslim community and in relation to which the Prophet is referred to as *ṣāḥib al-sharʿ* (trustee of the law). Many of the key terms discussed in the text such as, *ijtihād*, *takfīr*, *khilāfa*, *ikhtilāf* and *taqlīd* embody not only legal but communal concerns, further underscoring al-Ghazālī's conviction that the law is preserved and obeyed only through the life of the community – not just any community, but the *ahl al-sunna wa'l-jamāʿa*.

The opposing commitments of individualism and communalism are emblematic of the tensions in what, for want of a better term, we shall refer to as al-Ghazālī's personal conscience. His reaction to the implied individualism of the *taʿlīm* doctrine was, ironically, also what repeatedly attracted him to the doctrine, for al-Ghazālī himself displayed a remarkable individuality in his relationship to the community. This is persistently borne out through his accomplishments as an intellectual innovator, be it in his encounter with the *falāsifa*, reappraisal of *kalām*, systematic use of logic in *uṣūl al-fiqh*, and ultimately in his integration of Sufism within Sunni Islam. Al-Ghazālī's turning towards Sufism, which, if we recall, was to begin in earnest very soon after he had written the *K. al-Mustaẓhirī*, is perhaps the most articulate expression of his individualistic temperament, leading him to withdraw from the life of the community in order to pursue the dictates of his own personal conscience. Marshall Hodgson and Henri Laoust have both argued that the stirrings of what later developed into al-Ghazālī's existentialist posture (with the emphasis on religious experience) can be traced back to his engagement with the *taʿlīm* doctrine, especially since the *taʿlīm* doctrine, as much as al-Ghazālī would wish it to be underplayed, culminated in an act of existential commitment to, and dependence on, the teacher.[21] This interpretation brings to light one of the most fascinating ironies in Muslim intellectual history: that al-Ghazālī's intellectual reformation of Sunni Islam was in large part shaped by the ideas and ethos of the Shiʿa Ismaili doctrine of *taʿlīm.*

Al-Ghazālī's individualism never became an end unto itself, but persistently tempered itself to address and serve the needs of the community, as is reflected in the fact that his withdrawal from the community was short-lived, and after his return he continued to write and teach. His refutation of the *taʿlīm* doctrine and his concomitant adaptation of it, captures, albeit theoretically, the negotiation in his conscience between the attendant demands of individualistic commitment and communal (or contractual) participation. However, as noted earlier, evidence of this negotiation in the *K. al-Mustaẓhirī* is very much a part of the sub-text, though a sub-text which deserves attention not only because it anticipates the subsequent developments in al-Ghazālī's thought, but also because of the very significance of these ideas. This theme serves as a master key for understanding all of al-Ghazali's writings. Borrowing Isaiah Berlin's famous parable on thinkers as either hedgehogs (those affirming or desiring one big idea) or as foxes (those chasing many and even diverging ideas), I have come to see al-Ghazali as a restless and solitary fox, though one who yearned all his life to be a hedgehog.[22] Al-Ghazali's writings on all the major intellectual disciplines in medieval Islam display the tenacity of a remarkable fox, and yet all his wanderings seem driven by a hedgehog-like obsession for intellectual and communal consolidation. At the end of his thoughtful book on al-Ghazālī, Montgomery Watt aptly sums up his legacy:

> Above all he made the individualistic aspect of religion intellectually respectable. It is probably his emphasis on the individualistic outlook that has appealed to the endemic individualism of western scholars and gained him excessive praise; but he was far from being a sheer individualist. In his theorizing he sometimes fails to make explicit allowance for the communalism of the *sharīʿa,* but he always presupposes it, and in his practice he effects a genuine integration of individualism and communalism. This is part of his title to greatness and of his achievement in 'renewing' Islam.[23]

Though this study has focused ostensibly on re-reading the significance of al-Ghazali's debate with the Ismailis, it has sought also to illustrate, by way of this debate, the influential role played by Ismailis in the history of Islamic thought. Despite the renaissance of Ismaili studies over the past few decades through the writings of W. Ivanow, S.M. Stern, H. Corbin, M.G.S. Hodgson, W. Madelung, F. Daftary, P. Walker, A. Nanji, A. Asani and other scholars, there still abides a general perception of Ismaili thought as standing hermetically apart from, and on the margins of, Islamic civilization. This perception reflects simply a myopic understanding of the rich traffic of ideas and questions within Muslim intellectual life during the medieval era. The debate studied in this book provides us with a glimpse of the central intellectual tensions that were born out of that traffic, and to which Ismaili thinkers rendered some of the most original and significant contributions.

Notes

Preface

1. M.G.S. Hodgson, *The Venture of Islam: Conscience and History in a World Civilization* (Chicago, 1974), vol. 1, pp.71–99.

Chapter One: Ecology of the *Kitāb al-Mustaẓhirī*

1. I. Goldziher, *Die Streitschrift des Ghazālī gegen die Bātinijja-Sekte* (Leiden, 1916), pp.25–9; L. Massignon, *Recueil de texts inédits concernant l'histoire de la mystique aux pays d'Islam* (Paris, 1929), p.93; M. Asín Palacios, *La Espiritualidad de Algazel* (Madrid, 1935), vol. 1, pp.35–6; W.M. Watt, 'The Authenticity of the Works Attributed to al-Ghazālī', *Journal of the Royal Asiatic Society* (1952), pp.24–45; M. Bouyges, *Essai de chronologie des oeuvres de al-Ghazālī*, ed. M. Allard (Beirut, 1959); A. Badawi, *Mu'allafāt al-Ghazālī*, 2 vols. (Cairo, 1961); G.F. Hourani, 'The Chronology of Ghazālī's Writings', *Journal of the American Oriental Society*, 79 (1959), pp.225–33; see also his 'A Revised Chronology of Ghazālī's Writings', *Journal of the American Oriental Society*, 104 (1984), pp.284–302.

The recently-launched ambitious project of publishing critical editions with parallel English translations of al-Ghazālī's texts by Brigham Young University Press under its Islamic Translation Series, indicates the continuing level of interest in al-Ghazālī. The publications to date include editions and translations of *Tahāfut al-falāsifa* (*The Incoherence of the Philosophers*), ed. and trans. M. Marmura (Provo, Utah, 1997), and *Mishkāt al-anwār* (*The Niche of Lights*), ed. and trans. D. Buchman (Provo, Utah, 1998).

2. *Al-Munqidh min al-ḍalāl*, ed. F. Jabre (Beirut, 1959); see also R.J. McCarthy's annotated English translation, *Freedom and Fulfillment* (Boston, 1980).

3. Apart from a general discussion of this in W.M. Watt's admirable study, *Muslim Intellectual: A Study of al-Ghazālī* (Edinburgh, 1963), pp.171–80, see also the following perceptive articles on *al-Munqidh*: Josef van Ess, 'Quelques remarques sur le *Munqidh min al-ḍalāl*', in *Ghazālī: La raison et le miracle* (Paris, 1987), pp.56–68, and Eric L. Ormsby, 'The Taste of Truth: The Structure of Experience in al-Ghazālī's *al-Munqidh min al-ḍalāl*', in Wael B. Hallaq and Donald P. Little, ed., *Islamic Studies Presented to Charles J. Adams* (Leiden, 1991), pp.133–52.

4. A helpful reconstruction of the circumstances before and after al-Ghazālī's departure is contained in A.L. Tibawi, 'Al-Ghazālī's Sojourn in Damascus and Jerusalem', *Muslim World*, 9 (1965), pp.198–211.

5. Hourani, 'A Revised Chronology', pp.292–3.

6. Even a cursory list of all the significant monographs and articles by Claude Cahen on the Saljuqs would amount to no less than 20 items. A representative selection of his articles have been collected together in *Les Peuples musulmans dans l'histoire médiévale* (Damascus, 1977). Some of the titles in this collection consulted for this study include: 'The Historiography of the Seljukid Period', pp.36–64; 'L'Histoire économique et sociale de l'Orient musulman médiévale', pp.209–30; 'Nomades et Sidentaires dans le monde musulman du milieu du moyen âge', pp.423–37; and 'L'évolution de *l'iqṭāʿ* du IXe au XIIe siècle: contribution à une histoire comparée des sociétés médiévales', pp.231–70. See also Cahen's 'Mouvements populaires et autonomisme urban dans l'Asie musulman du moyen âge', *Arabica*, 5 (1958), pp.225–50; 'The Turkish Invasion: The Selchükids', in K.M. Setton, ed., *A History of the Crusades* (rev. ed. Madison, Wisconsin, 1964), vol. 1. pp.135–76; 'Tribes, Cities, and Social Organization', in *The Cambridge History of Iran*: Volume 4, *The Period from the Arab Invasion to the Saljuqs*, ed. R.N. Frye (Cambridge, 1975), pp.308–28. For a more accessible and general summary of his views consult his *Pre-Ottoman Turkey*, tr. J. Jones-Williams (London, 1968).

7. Once again, the entirety of Lambton's and Makdisi's contributions on the subject would be far too numerous to cite here. Lambton's major writings include: *Landlord and Peasant in Persia: A Study of Land*

Tenure and Land Revenue Administration (2nd ed., London, 1969); *Continuity and Change in Medieval Persia: Aspects of Administrative, Economic, and Social History, 11th-14th Century* (Albany, NY, 1988). See also her equally significant articles 'The Internal Structure of the Saljuq Empire', in *The Cambridge History of Iran*: Volume 5, *The Saljuq and Mongol Periods*, ed. J.A. Boyle (Cambridge, 1968), pp.203–82; 'Reflections on the *Iqṭā*ʿ, in G. Makdisi, ed., *Arabic and Islamic Studies in Honor of Hamilton A.R. Gibb* (Cambridge, MA, 1965), pp.358–76. As for Makdisi, his research bears witness to an ambitious (revisionist, if you will) line of enquiry. Beginning with 'Muslim Institutions of Learning in Eleventh Century Baghdad', *Bulletin of the School of Oriental and African Studies*, 24 (1961), pp.1–56, thereafter complemented by a spate of related articles, significant among which: 'Ashʿarī and the Ashʿarites in Islamic Religious History', *Studia Islamica*, 17 (1962), pp.37–80, 18 (1963), pp.19–40; 'The Sunni Revival', in D.S. Richards, ed., *Islamic Civilisation, 950–1150* (Oxford, 1973), pp.155–68, then culminating in his exemplary study *The Rise of Colleges: Institutions of Learning in Islam and the West* (Edinburgh, 1981). The conclusions of this last study have been further assessed in 'The Juridical Theology of Shāfiʿī: Origins and Significance of *Uṣūl al-fiqh*', *Studia Islamica*, 59 (1984), pp.5–48, and in what is perhaps his greatest scholarly achievement, *The Rise of Humanism in Classical Islam and the Christian West: With Special Reference to Scholasticism* (Edinburgh, 1990), pp.2–43.

8. C.E. Bosworth, 'Barbarian Invasions: The Coming of the Turks into the Islamic World', in Richards, ed., *Islamic Civilisation*, p.1.

9. Roy P. Mottahedeh, 'The Abbasid Caliphate in Iran', *The Cambridge History of Iran*: Volume 4, pp.60–75.

10. H. Busse, 'The Revival of Persian Kingship under the Buyids', in Richards, ed., *Islamic Civilisation*, pp.47–69.

11. See C. Cahen, 'Historiography of the Seljuqid Period', pp.39–43, and C.E. Bosworth, 'The Political and Dynastic History of the Iranian World (AD 1000–1217)', in *The Cambridge History of Iran*: Volume 5, pp.44–9.

12. See in particular Lambton, 'The Internal Structure of the Saljuq Empire', pp.203–25.

13. Makdisi, 'The Sunni Revival', pp.168.

14. As mentioned earlier, this is recapitulated comprehensively in Makdisi's *The Rise of Colleges.*

15. Summarized succinctly in Makdisi, *The Rise of Humanism*, pp.2–15.

16. Makdisi, *The Rise of Colleges*, pp.281–91.
17. Makdisi, *The Rise of Humanism*, pp.24–9.
18. Ibid., pp.40–1.
19. Makdisi, 'The Juridical Theology of Shāfiʿī', *Studia Islamica*, 59 (1984), pp.43–4.
20. Watt, *A Muslim Intellectual*, pp.20–3.
21. Ibid., p.23.
22. Bosworth, 'Political and Dynastic History', pp.102–9.
23. H.A.R. Gibb, 'Al-Māwardī's Theory of the Caliphate', in Stanford J. Shaw and William R. Polk, ed., *Studies on the Civilization of Islam* (Boston, 1962), pp.151–65.
24. Bosworth, 'Political and Dynastic History', pp.100–2.
25. A fascinating reconstruction of this whole episode can be found in G. Makdisi, 'The Marriage of Tughril Beg', *International Journal of Middle East Studies*, 1 (1970), pp.259–75.
26. Niẓām al-Mulk, *Siyāsat-nāma*, English tr. Herbert Drake, *The Book of Government or Rules for Kings* (2nd ed. London, 1978), pp.9–13.
27. Bosworth, 'Political and Dynastic History', pp.106–7.
28. G. Makdisi, 'The Topography of Eleventh Century Baghdad', *Arabica*, 6 (1959), pp.290–305.
29. Ibid., pp.292–5.
30. Ibid., pp.303.
31. Bosworth, 'Political and Dynastic History', pp.106–7.
32. G. Makdisi, 'Authority in the Islamic Community', in G. Makdisi, ed., *La Notion d'autorité au moyen âge: Islam, Byzance, Occident* (Paris, 1982), p.122.
33. Farhad Daftary, *The Ismāʿīlīs: Their History and Doctrines* (Cambridge, 1990), p.262, and his 'Ḥasan-i Ṣabbāḥ and the Origins of the Nizārī Ismaʿili Movement', in F. Daftary, ed., *Mediaeval Ismaʿili History and Thought* (Cambridge, 1996), pp.181–204.
34. Marius Canard, 'Fāṭimids', *EI2*, vol. 2, pp.850–62; Daftary, *The Ismāʿīlīs*, pp.224–32.
35. An interesting analysis of this is in Marshall G.S. Hodgson, *The Order of Assassins: The Struggle of the Early Nizārī Ismāʿīlīs Against the Islamic World* (The Hague, 1955), pp.41–8.
36. Daftary, *The Ismāʿīlīs*, pp.212–15, pp.224–32; for a more detailed description see Abbas Hamdani, 'Evolution of the Organisational Structure of the Fāṭimī Daʿwah', *Arabian Studies*, 3 (1976), pp.85–114, and Heinz Halm, *The Fatimids and their Traditions of Learning* (London, 1997).

37. W. Madelung, 'The Sources of Ismā'īlī Law', *Journal of Near Eastern Studies*, 35 (1976), pp.29–40, reprinted in W. Madelung, *Religious Schools and Sects in Medieval Islam* (London, 1985), article xviii.

38. Many legends have been woven around the figure of the Nizārī *fidā'ī*, dating back to some of the twelfth-century European chroniclers of the Crusades and the writings of European travellers, the most popular of which is the late thirteenth-century account of the Venetian, Marco Polo (d.1324). Apart from caricaturing the fanatical devotion of these *fidā'īs* as a group of manipulated martyrs under the influence of the drug hashish, these legends have been responsible for coining and introducing the term 'assassin' into European languages. The most comprehensive analysis of this development is in Daftary, *The Ismā'īlīs*, pp.4–21; and his *The Assassin Legends: Myths of the Ismailis* (London, 1994).

39. A sympathetic, yet no less suggestive, interpretation of these assassinations is in Hodgson, *The Order of Assassins*, pp.79–89; see also Daftary, *The Ismā'īlīs*, p.342.

40. Niẓām al-Mulk, *The Book of Government*, pp.208–31.

41. Muḥammad b. 'Abd al-Karīm al-Shahrastānī, *Kitāb al-Milal wa'l-niḥal* (London, 1846), pp.92–3; partial English trans. by A.K. Kazi and J.G. Flynn, *Muslim Sects and Divisions* (London, 1984), pp.167–70.

42. The titles of the two extant texts of al-Ghazālī as cited in Hourani, 'Revised Chronology', are *Qawāsim al-Bāṭiniyya*, ed. A. Ates, in *Ilāhiyat Fakultesi Dergisi*, 3 (Istanbul, 1954), pp.23–54 and *Al-Qiṣṭās al-mustaqīm*, ed. V. Chelhot, (Beirut, 1959); while the titles of the two lost texts are *Hujjat al-ḥaqq* and *Kitāb al-Darj*.

43. For a general, yet perceptive, discussion of *ẓann* in Islamic Law see Bernard Weiss, 'Interpretation in Islamic Law: The Theory of *Ijtihād*', *American Journal of Comparative Law*, 26 (1978), pp.203–7.

Chapter Two: Anatomy of the *Kitāb al-Mustaẓhirī*

1. Leo Strauss, *Persecution and the Art of Writing* (Glencoe, IL, 1952), p.143.

2. Ibid.

3. The terms 'Bāṭiniyya' and 'Ta'līmiyya' which al-Ghazālī uses in a pejorative sense for the Ismailis will occasionally be retained in the analysis that follows in order to provide a flavour of his polemical style.

4. Al-Ghazālī, translation p.176; text p.2. Henceforth throughout the notes, all quotations from and references to the *Kitāb al-Mustaẓhirī*

will be cited first with reference to the English translation of the text in Richard Joseph McCarthy, *Freedom and Fulfillment* (Boston, 1980), pp.175–286, and then to the critical edition of the Arabic text by ʿAbd al-Raḥmān Badawī, *Faḍā'iḥ al-Bāṭiniyya wa faḍā'il al-Mustaẓhiriyya* (Cairo, 1383/1964). Almost all the passages cited in this study have followed McCarthy's translation, with, at times, some minor adaptations or re-working. Of the two sets of pagination cited, the first refers to McCarthy's translation and the second to Badawi's Arabic edition; if there is only one page reference cited, it refers to the Arabic edition alone.

5. Al-Ghazālī, p.178; p.5.
6. Ibid., p.179; p.6.
7. Ibid., p.177; p.2.
8. Ibid.
9. Ibid., p.177, p.179; p.4, p.6.
10. Ibid., p.176; p.2.
11. Ibid., p.177; pp.3–4.
12. Ibid., pp.177–8; p.4.
13. Ibid., pp.179–81; pp.7–9.
14. Ibid., p.180; p.8.
15. The most thorough and discerning review of the heresiographical tradition in Islam is to be found in the writings of W.M. Watt; see his *The Formative Period of Islamic Thought* (Edinburgh, 1973), pp.1–9, and 'The Great Community and the Sects', in G.E. von Grunebaum, ed., *Theology and the Law in Islam* (Wiesbaden 1971), pp.25–36. A thoughtful examination of the subject is also contained in Bernard Lewis, 'Some Observations on the Significance of Heresy in the History of Islam', *Studia Islamica*, 1 (1953), pp.43–63.
16. Watt, 'The Great Community', p.25.
17. Ibid., p.26.
18. Al-Ghazālī, p.222; p.78.
19. Ibid., p.183; p.17.
20. Ibid.
21. Ibid., p.184; p.20.
22. Ibid., p.195; p.37.
23. Ibid., p.208; p.55.
24. Ibid., p.193; p.33.
25. Ibid., pp.185–92; pp.21–32. For a broader discussion of al-Ghazālī's endeavour to deliberately misinterpret the Ismailis, see Henry Corbin, 'The Ismāʿīlī Response to the Polemic of Ghazālī', in S.H. Nasr,

ed., *Ismāʿīlī Contributions to Islamic Culture* (Tehran, 1977), pp.67–98.

26. References to these texts as quoted by Daftary, *The Ismāʿīlīs*, p.92. A critical edition and English translation of the *Kitāb al-ʿālim wa'l-ghulām* has been prepared by James W. Morris under the title *The Master and the Disciple: An Early Islamic Spiritual Dialogue* (London, forthcoming).

27. Al-Ghazālī, p.185; p.21.

28. Ibid., p.192; p.32.

29. Ibid.,pp.192–5; pp.33–6.

30. Ibid., p.192; p.33.

31. Ibid., p.195; p.37.

32. Ibid., p.192, pp.195–6; p.33, pp.37–8.

33. Ibid., pp.218, 275; 72, 164.

34. Makdisi, *The Rise of Humanism*, pp.7–9; an English translation of the creed appears in Adam Mez, *The Renaissance of Islam*, English tr., S. Khuda Bakhsh and D.S. Margoliouth (New York, 1975), pp.206–9.

35. Al-Ghazālī, p.196; p.38.

36. Ibid., pp.196–7; pp.38–40.

37. For a discussion of this aspect of Fatimid thought see Paul E. Walker, 'An Ismāʿīlī Answer to the Problem of Worshipping the Unknowable, Neoplatonic God', *American Journal of Arabic Studies*, 2 (1974), pp.7–21; Wilferd Madelung, 'Aspects of Ismāʿīlī Theology: The Prophetic Chain and the God Beyond Being', in Nasr, ed., *Ismāʿīlī Contributions to Islamic Culture*, pp.51–65; and Mohamed A. Alibhai, 'Abū Yaʿqūb al-Sijistānī and Kitāb Sullam al-Najāt' (Ph.D. thesis, Harvard University, 1983), pp.65–84.

38. Al-Ghazālī, p.197; p.40.

39. Ibid.

40. Ibid., pp.198; pp.40–2.

41. Ibid., p.198; p.42.

42. Ibid., pp.198–200; pp.42–5.

43. Ibid., p.200; p.44.

44. A summary of this debate can be found in Oliver Leaman, *Introduction to Medieval Islamic Philosophy* (Cambridge, 1985), pp.25–59.

45. Al-Ghazālī, pp.200–1; pp.44–6.

46. Ibid., p.202; p.46.

47. Ibid.

48. Ibid., pp.202; pp.46–7.

49. Ibid.
50. Ibid.
51. Ibid., p.203, p.206; p.48, pp.51–2.
52. Ibid., pp.206–7; pp.52–3.
53. Ibid., p.208; pp.55–6.
54. Ibid., pp.208–15; pp.55–65.
55. Ibid., p.211; p.60.
56. Ibid., pp.211–12; pp.60–1.
57. Ibid., pp.212–15; pp.61–6.
58. Ibid., p.213; p.62
59. Ibid., p.218; p.73.
60. Ibid., p.222; p.79.
61. For al-Ghazālī this would have meant al-Mustanṣir (*d.*487/1094), as it does not seem that he was aware of the succession dispute around the latter's son Nizar.
62. Ibid., p.218; p.73.
63. Ibid., pp.218–20; pp.73–5.
64. Josef van Ess, 'The Logical Structure of Islamic Theology', in G.E. von Grunebaum, ed., *Logic in Classical Islamic Culture* (Wiesbaden, 1970), pp.46–8.
65. Al-Shahrastānī, *al-Milal wa'l-niḥal*, pp.92–4; English tr., *Muslim Sects and Divisions*, pp.167–70.
66. Ibid., p.93; p.169.
67. Hodgson, *The Venture of Islam*, vol. 2, p.185.
68. Al-Shahrastānī, *al-Milal wa'l-niḥal*, p.93; English tr., *Muslim Sects and Divisions*, p.169.
69. Henry Corbin, 'The Ismāʿīlī Response to the Polemic of Ghazālī', pp.71–2.
70. Al-Ghazālī, p.220; p.76.
71. Ibid., pp.220–1; p.76.
72. Ibid., p.221; p.77.
73. Ibid.
74. Ibid., p.222; p.78.
75. Ibid., p.222; pp.78–9.
76. Ibid., p.222; p.79.
77. Ibid.
78. Ibid., p.223; p.80.
79. Ibid., p.224; p.81.
80. Ibid.
81. Ibid., p.225; p.83.

82. Ibid., p.223; p.80.
83. Ibid., p.227; pp.85–6.
84. Ibid.
85. Ibid., pp.228–9; pp.87–8.
86. Ibid., p.228; p.87.
87. Ibid., p.229; p.87.
88. A thorough examination of these issues can be found in Wael B. Hallaq, 'On Inductive Corroboration, Probability, and Certainty in Sunnī Legal Thought', in Nicholas Heer, ed., *Islamic Law and Jurisprudence: Studies in Honour of Farhat J. Ziadeh* (Seattle, 1990), pp.6–21.
89. Al-Ghazālī, p.229; p.88.
90. Ibid., p.230; p.89.
91. Ibid.
92. Ibid., 250, pp.260–1; pp.129–30.
93. Ibid., pp.234–9; pp.95–102.
94. Ibid., p.250; p.116.
95. Ibid., p.238; p.100.
96. Ibid., p.235; p.95.
97. Ibid., pp.261–4; pp.132–46.
98. Ibid., pp.265–74; pp.146–68.
99. Ibid., p.262; p.135.
100. Ibid., p.262; p.136.
101. Ibid., p.262; pp.136–7.
102. Hallaq, 'On Inductive Corroboration, Probability, and Certainty in Sunnī Legal Thought', p.10.
103. Al-Ghazālī, p.264; p.144.
104. Ibid., p.265; p.146.
105. This text has also been translated by Richard J. McCarthy in *Freedom and Fulfillment*, pp.145–74; an extremely lucid analysis of it is in Toshihiko Izutsu, *The Concept of Belief in Islamic Theology: A Semantic Analysis of Imān and Islām* (Tokyo, 1965), pp.23–34.
106. Al-Ghazālī, p.265; pp.146–7.
107. Ibid., pp.265–6; pp.146–7.
108. Ibid., p.265; p.147.
109. Ibid., p.266; p.144.
110. Ibid., p.267; pp.152–3.
111. Ibid., p.267; pp.153–4.
112. Ibid., pp.267–8; pp.154–5.
113. Ibid., p.268; p.155.
114. Ibid., p.268; pp.156–7.

115. Ibid., pp.268–74; pp.157–68.
116. Erwin Rosenthal, *Political Thought in Medieval Islam* (Cambridge, 1962), p.38; A.K.S. Lambton, *State and Government in Medieval Islam* (Oxford, 1981), p.110; Carole Hillenbrand, 'Islamic Orthodoxy or Realpolitik? Al-Ghazālī's Views on Government', in *Iran: Journal of the British Institute of Persian Studies*, 26 (1988), pp.81–3.
117. Henri Laoust, *La Politique de Gazālī* (Paris, 1970), pp.56–83.
118. Gibb, 'Al-Māwardī's Theory of the Caliphate', p.162.
119. Al-Ghazālī, p.274; p.169.
120. Ibid.
121. Ibid., pp.274–5; pp.169–70.
122. Ibid., p.275; p.170.
123. Ibid., pp.170–2; Gibb, 'Al-Mawardi's Theory of the Caliphate', p.155.
124. Al-Ghazālī, pp.171–2.
125. Ibid., pp.170–3.
126. Ibid., p.276; p.172.
127. Ibid., p.276; p.173.
128. Hillenbrand, 'Islamic Orthodoxy or Realpolitik?', pp.87–90. See also Leonard Binder, 'Al-Ghazālī's Theory of Government', *Muslim World*, 45, (1955), pp.233–40.
129. Hillenbrand, 'Islamic Orthodoxy or Realpolitik?', pp.83–6.
130. A succinct review of these developments can be found in Bernard Lewis, 'Politics and War', in J. Schacht and C.E. Bosworth, ed., *The Legacy of Islam* (2nd ed., Oxford, 1974), pp.161–4.
131. Hillenbrand, 'Islamic Orthodoxy or Realpolitik?', pp.85–7.
132. Al-Ghazālī, pp.175–6.
133. Ibid., p.277; p.177.
134. Ibid., pp.176–7; Hillenbrand, 'Islamic Orthodoxy or Realpolitik?', p.83.
135. Al-Ghazālī, p.277; p.178.
136. Ibid., p.278; pp.180–1.
137. Ibid., p.180.
138. Ibid., p.183; Hillenbrand, 'Islamic Orthodoxy or Realpolitik?', p.83.
139. Al-Ghazālī, p.183.
140. Ibid., p.185; Qur'an 5:19.
141. Al-Ghazālī, p.186.
142. Ibid., pp.187–90.
143. Ibid., p.278; p.191.

144. Ibid., p.279; p.191.
145. Ibid., p.279; pp.193–4.
146. Ibid.
147. Hillenbrand, 'Islamic Orthodoxy or Realpolitik?', pp.91–2.
148. Al-Ghazālī, pp.195–200.
149. Ibid., pp.212–20.
150. Hillenbrand, 'Islamic Orthodoxy or Realpolitik?', p.93.
151. *Ghiyāth al-umam*, by al-Juwaynī, ed. F. 'Abd al-Mun'im and M. Hilmi (Alexandria, 1979).
152. Wael Hallaq, 'Caliphs, Jurists and the Saljuqs in the Political Thought of Juwaynī', *Muslim World*, 74 (1984), pp.26–41.

Chapter Three: Towards a Re-reading of the *Kitāb al-Mustaẓhirī*

1. As quoted in G. Makdisi, 'Ḥanbalite Islam', in M.L. Swartz, ed., *Studies on Islam* (New York, 1981), pp.251–2.
2. Al-Ghazālī, pp.259–61; pp.128–30.
3. See, in particular, Makdisi's 'Ash'arī and the Ash'arites in Islamic Religious History', pp.25–40; 'Ḥanbalite Islam', pp.262–4; and 'The Juridical Theology of Shāfi'ī', pp.40–7.
4. Bernard Weiss, 'Law in Islam and in the West: Some Comparative Observations', in Wael B. Hallaq and Donald P. Little, ed., *Islamic Studies Presented to Charles J. Adams* (Leiden, 1991), pp.242–5.
5. For Wael B. Hallaq, see in particular 'Logic, Formal Arguments and Formalization of Arguments in Sunnī Jurisprudence', *Arabica*, 37 (1990), pp.315–58; 'On Inductive Corroboration, Probability and Certainty in Sunnī Legal Thought', pp.6–31; and *A History of Islamic Legal Theories* (Cambridge, 1997). For Richard M. Frank see in particular his 'Al-Ash'arī's Conception of the Nature and Role of Speculative Reasoning in Theology', in Frithiof Rungren, ed., *Proceedings of the Sixth Congress of Arabic and Islamic Studies* (Stockholm, 1975), pp.136–54; *Beings and Their Attributes* (Albany, NY, 1978); 'The Science of *kalām*', *Arabic Science and Philosophy*, 2 (1992), pp.9–37; and more recently his revisionist ideas in *Al-Ghazālī and the Ash'arite School* (Durham, NC, 1994).
6. Josef van Ess, 'Scepticism in Islamic Religious Thought', in C. Malik, ed., *God and Man in Contemporary Islamic Thought* (Beirut, 1972), p.97.

7. Ibid., pp.95–7.

8. Mohammed Arkoun, 'The Concept of Authority in Islamic Thought: *Lā ḥukma illā lillāh*', in C.E. Bosworth et al., ed., *The Islamic World from Classical to Modern Times: Essays in Honor of Bernard Lewis* (Princeton, NJ, 1989), pp.31–5.

9. Ibid., pp.34–7.

10. Max Weber, *From Max Weber: Essays in Sociology*, eds. H.H. Gerth and C.W. Mills (New York, 1959), pp.50–75; Hamid Dabashi, *Authority in Islam: From the Rise of Muhammad to the Establishment of the Ummayads* (New Brunswick, NJ, 1989), pp.71–120.

11. Al-Ghazālī, pp.143–5, pp.169–70, pp.195–6.

12. W.M. Watt, 'Authority in the Thought of al-Ghazālī', in G. Makdisi, ed., *La Notion d'autorité au moyen âge: Islam, Byzance, Occident* (Paris, 1982), p.60.

13. Aziz Al-Azmeh, *Arabic Thought and Islamic Societies* (London, 1986), p.260.

14. Ibid. See also R. Stephen Humphreys, *Islamic History: A Framework for Inquiry* (London, 1991), pp.187–208.

15. Al-Ghazālī, pp.87–9, p.95, pp.191–4.

16. Al-Ghazālī, pp.87–9. For a broader discussion of this see the thought-provoking study by Hermann Landolt, 'Ghazālī and *Religionwissenschaft*', *Asiatische Studien - Etudes Asiatiques*, 45 (1991), pp.19–23.

17. Al-Ghazālī, *al-Munqidh min al-ḍalāl*, ed. F. Jabre (Beirut, 1959).

18. A perceptive discussion of this text can be found in Hallaq, 'Logic, Formal Arguments and Formalization', pp.336–58, which contains an annotated translation of al-Ghazālī's introduction to the text; see also his '*Uṣūl al-Fiqh*: Beyond Tradition', *Journal of Islamic Studies*, 3 (1992), pp.188–91.

19. Hodgson, *The Venture of Islam*, vol. 2, p.184.

20. Hodgson, *The Order of Assassins*, pp.126–31; his *The Venture of Islam*, vol. 2, pp.183–4; Watt, *Muslim Intellectual*, pp.82–6.

21. Hodgson, *The Venture of Islam*, vol. 2, pp.183–92. Laoust, *La Politique de Gazālī*, pp.75–94.

22. Isaiah Berlin, 'The Hedgehog and the Fox', in H. Hardy, ed., *Russian Thinkers* (London, 1978) pp.22–81.

23. Watt, *Muslim Intellectual*, p.180.

Bibliography

Alibhai, Mohamed A. 'Abū Ya'qūb al-Sijistānī and Kitāb Sullam al-Najāt', Ph.D. thesis, Harvard University, 1983.

Anawati, G.C. and Louis Gardet. *Introduction à la théologie Musulmane: essai de théologie comparée.* Paris, 1970.

Arkoun, Mohammed. 'The Concept of Authority in Islamic Thought: *Lā ḥukma illā lillāh*', in C.E. Bosworth et al., ed., *The Islamic World from Classical to Modern Times: Essays in Honor of Bernard Lewis,* Princeton, NJ, 1989, pp.31–54.

——*Rethinking Islam Today.* Washington, 1987.

al-Ash'arī, Abu'l-Ḥasan. *Kitāb maqālāt al-islāmiyyīn,* ed. H. Ritter. Istanbul, 1929–1930.

Al-Azmeh, Aziz. *Arabic Thought and Islamic Societies.* London, 1986.

Badawī, 'Abd al-Raḥmān. *Mu'allafāt al-Ghazālī.* Cairo, 1961.

al-Baghdādī, 'Abd al-Qāhir. *al-Farq bayn al-firaq,* ed. M. Badr. Cairo, 1910. English tr., part 1, K.C. Seelye, *Moslem Schisms and Sects,* New York, 1919.

Binder, Leonard. 'Al-Ghazālī's Theory of Government', *Muslim World,* 45, (1955), pp.233–40.

Bosworth, C. Edmund. 'The Political and Dynastic History of the Iranian World (AD 1000–1217)', in *The Cambridge History of Iran: Volume 5, The Saljuq and Mongol Periods,* ed. J.A. Boyle. Cambridge, 1968, pp.1–202.

——'Barbarian Invasions: The Coming of the Turks into the Islamic World', in D.S. Richards, ed., *Islamic Civilisation,* pp.1–16.

Bouyges, M. *Essai de chronologie des oeuvres de al-Ghazālī*, ed. M. Allard. Beirut, 1959.

Busse, H. 'The Revival of Persian Kingship under the Buyids', in D.S. Richards, ed., *Islamic Civilisation*, pp.47–69.

Cahen, Claude. 'L'Évolution de *l'iqṭāʿ* du IXe au XIIe siècle: contribution à une histoire comparée des sociétés médiévales', in *Les Peuples musulmans dans l'histoire médiévale*. Damascus, 1977, pp.231–70.

——'Mouvements populaires et autonomisme urban dans l'Asie musulmane du moyen âge', *Arabica*, 5 (1958), pp.225–50.

——'The Turkish Invasion: The Selchükids', in *A History of the Crusades*, ed. K.M. Setton: Volume 1, *The First Hundred Years*, ed. M.W. Baldwin. 2nd ed., Madison, Wisconsin, 1969, pp.175–6.

——'Tribes, Cities, and Social Organization', in *The Cambridge History of Iran*: Volume 4, *The Period from the Arab Invasion to the Saljuqs*, ed. R.N. Frye. Cambridge, 1975, pp.308–28.

——*Pre-Ottoman Turkey*, tr. J. James-Williams. London, 1968.

——*Les Peuples musulmans dans l'histoire médiévale*. Damascus, 1977.

Calder, Norman. 'The Limits of Islamic Orthodoxy', in F. Daftary, ed., *Intellectual Traditions in Islam*. London, 2000, pp.66–86.

Canard, Marius. 'Fāṭimids', *EI2*, vol. 2, pp.850–62.

Corbin, Henry. 'The Ismāʿīlī Response to the Polemic of Ghazālī', in S.H. Nasr, ed., *Ismāʿīlī Contributions to Islamic Culture*. Tehran, 1977, pp.67–98.

——*History of Islamic Philosophy*, tr. L. Sherrard. London, 1993.

Dabashi, Hamid. *Authority in Islam: From the Rise of Muhammad to the Establishment of the Umayyads*. New Brunswick, NJ, 1989.

Daftary, Farhad. *The Ismāʿīlīs: Their History and Doctrines*. Cambridge, 1990.

——*The Assassin Legends: Myths of the Ismaʿilis*. London, 1994.

——ed., *Mediaeval Ismaʿili History and Thought*. Cambridge, 1996.

——'The Ismaili *Daʿwa* outside the Fatimid *Dawla*', in M. Barrucand, ed., *L'Egypte Fatimide, son art et son histoire*. Paris, 1999, pp.29–43.

Djait, Hichem. *Europe and Islam: Cultures and Modernity*. Berkeley, CA, 1985.

Eliot, T.S. 'Tradition and the Individual Talent', in Frank Kermode, ed., *Selected Prose of T.S. Eliot*. London, 1975, pp.37–44.

Esmail, Aziz. *The Poetics of Religious Experience: The Islamic Context*. London, 1988.

Ess, Josef, van. 'The Logical Structure of Islamic Theology', in G.E. von

Grunebaum, ed., *Logic in Classical Islamic Culture*. Wiesbaden, 1970, pp.21–50.
——'Scepticism in Islamic Religious Thought', in C. Malik, ed., *God and Man in Contemporary Islamic Thought*. Beirut, 1972, pp.83–98.
——'Quelques remarques sur le *Munqidh min al-ḍalāl*', in *Ghazālī: La raison et le miracle*. Paris, 1987, pp.56–68.
Frank, Richard M. 'Al-Ashʿarī's Conception of the Nature and Role of Speculative Reasoning in Theology', in Frithiof Rugren, ed., *Proceedings of the Sixth Congress of Arabic and Islamic Studies*. Stockholm, 1975, pp.136–54.
——*Beings and Their Attributes*. Albany, NY, 1978.
——'The Science of *kalām*', *Arabic Science and Philosophy*, 2 (1992), pp.9–37.
——*Al-Ghazālī and the Ashʿarite School*. Durham, NC, 1994.
al-Ghazālī, Abū Ḥāmid Muḥammad. *Faḍā'iḥ al-Bāṭiniyya wa faḍā'il al-Mustaẓhiriyya*, ed. ʿAbd al-Raḥmān Badawī. Cairo, 1964. English tr. Richard J. McCarthy in *Freedom and Fulfillment*. Boston, 1980, pp.175–286.
——*Fayṣal al-tafriqa bayn al-Islām wa'l-zandaqa*, ed. Sulayman Dunya. Cairo, 1961.
——*al-Iqtiṣād fi'l-iʿtiqād*, ed. I.A. Çubukcu and H. Atay. Ankara, 1962.
——*al-Mustaṣfā min ʿilm al-uṣūl*, ed. Muḥammad ʿAbd al-Salām al-Thānī. Beirut, 1993.
——*Mishkāt al-anwār*, English tr. David Buchman, *The Niche of Lights*. Provo, Utah, 1998.
——*al-Munqidh min al-ḍalāl*, ed. Farid Jabre. Beirut, 1959. English tr. Richard J. McCarthy in *Freedom and Fulfillment*. Boston, 1980, pp.61–115.
——*Naṣīḥat al-mulūk*, English tr. F.R.C. Bagely, *Ghazālī's Book of Counsel for Kings*. Oxford, 1964.
——*Qawāsim al-Bāṭiniyya*, ed. A. Ates, in *Ilāhiyat Fakultesi Dergisi*, 3 (1954), pp.23–54.
——*al-Qiṣṭās al-mustaqīm*, ed. V. Chelot. Beirut, 1959. English tr. Richard J. McCarthy in *Freedom and Fulfillment*. Boston, 1980, pp.287–333.
——*Tahāfut al-falāsifa*, English tr. Michael E. Marmura, *The Incoherence of the Philosophers*. Provo, Utah, 1997.
Gibb, Hamilton A.R. 'Al-Mawardi's Theory of the Caliphate', in S.J.

Shaw and W.R. Polk, ed., *Studies on the Civilisation of Islam.* Boston, 1962, pp.151–65.

Goldziher, Ignaz. *Die Streitschrift des Ghazālī gegen die Bāṭinijja-Sekte.* Leiden, 1916.

Hallaq, Wael B. 'Caliphs, Jurists and the Saljuqs in the Political Thought of Juwaynī', *Muslim World,* 74 (1984), pp.26–41.

——'On Inductive Corroboration, Probability, and Certainty in Sunnī Legal Thought', in Nicholas Heer, ed., *Islamic Law and Jurisprudence: Studies in Honour of Farhat J. Ziadeh.* Seattle, 1990, pp.6–31.

——'Logic, Formal Arguments and Formalization of Arguments in Sunnī Jurisprudence', *Arabica,* 37 (1990), pp.315–58.

——'The Primacy of the Qur'an in Shātibī's Legal Theory', in Wael B. Hallaq and Donald P. Little, ed., *Islamic Studies Presented to Charles J. Adams.* Leiden, 1991, pp.69–90.

——'*Uṣūl al-Fiqh*: Beyond Tradition', *Journal of Islamic Studies,* 3 (1992), pp.172–202.

——*Ibn Taymiyya Against The Greek Logicians.* Oxford, 1993.

——*Law and Legal Theory in Classical and Medieval Islam.* Aldershot, 1995.

——*A History of Islamic Legal Theories.* Cambridge, 1997.

Halm, Heinz. *The Fatimids and their Traditions of Learning.* London, 1997.

Hamdani, Abbas. *The Beginnings of the Ismāʿīlī Daʿwa in Northern India.* Cairo, 1956.

——'Evolution of the Organisational Structure of the Fāṭimī Daʿwah', *Arabian Studies,* 3 (1976), pp.85–114.

——'The Ṭayyibī-Fāṭimid Community of the Yaman at the Time of the Ayyūbid Conquest of Southern Arabia', *Arabian Studies,* 7 (1985), pp.151–60.

Hillenbrand, Carole. 'Islamic Orthodoxy or Realpolitik? Al-Ghazālī's Views on Government', in *Iran: Journal of the British Institute of Persian Studies,* 26 (1988), pp.81–94.

——'The Power Struggle between the Saljuqs and the Ismaʿilis of Alamūt: The Saljuq Perspective', in F. Daftary, ed., *Mediaeval Ismaʿili History and Thought.* Cambridge, 1996, pp.205–20.

Hodgson, Marshall G.S. *The Order of Assassins: The Struggle of the Early Nizārī Ismāʿīlīs Against the Islamic World.* The Hague, 1955.

——'The Ismāʿīlī State', in *The Cambridge History of Iran:* Volume 5, *The Saljuq and Mongol Periods,* ed. J.A. Boyle. Cambridge, 1968, pp.422–82.

——*The Venture of Islam: Conscience and History in a World Civilization.* Chicago, 1974.

Hourani, George F. 'The Chronology of Ghazālī's Writings', *Journal of the American Oriental Society,* 79 (1959), pp.225–33.

——'A Revised Chronology of Ghazālī's Writings', *Journal of the American Oriental Society,* 104 (1984), pp.284–302.

Humphreys, R. Stephen. *Islamic History: A Framework for Inquiry.* Rev. ed., London, 1991.

Hunsberger, Alice C. *Nasir Khusraw: The Ruby of Badakhshan.* London, 2000.

Ivanow, Wladimir. *Ismaili Literature: A Bibliographical Survey.* Tehran, 1963.

Izutsu, Toshihiko. *The Concept of Belief in Islamic Theology: A Semantic Analysis of Imān and Islām.* Tokyo, 1965.

Ja'far b. Manṣūr al-Yaman. *Kitāb al-ʿĀlim wa'l-ghulām,* ed. and English tr., James W. Morris, *The Master and the Disciple: An Early Islamic Spiritual Dialogue.* London, forthcoming.

al-Juwaynī. *Ghiyāth al-umam,* ed. F. 'Abd al-Munʿim and M. Hilmi. Alexandria, 1979.

Lambton, Ann K.S. 'Reflections on the *Iqtāʿ*,' in George Makdisi, ed., *Arabic and Islamic Studies in Honor of Hamilton A.R. Gibb.* Cambridge, MA, 1965, pp.358–75.

——'The Internal Structure of the Saljuq Empire', in *The Cambridge History of Iran:* Volume 5. *The Saljuq and Mongol Periods,* ed. J.A. Boyle. Cambridge, 1968, pp.203–82.

——*Landlord and Peasant in Persia: A Study of Land Tenure and Land Revenue Administration.* 2nd. ed., London, 1969.

——*State and Government in Medieval Islam.* Oxford, 1981.

——*Continuity and Change in Medieval Persia: Aspects of Administrative, Economic, and Social History, 11–14th Century.* Albany, NY, 1988.

Landolt, Hermann. 'Ghazālī and *Religionswissenschaft*', *Asiatische Studien-Etudes Asiatiques,* 45 (1991) pp.19–72.

Laoust, Henri. *La Politique de Gazālī.* Paris, 1970.

Lazarus-Yafeh, H. *Studies in al-Ghazzālī.* Jerusalem, 1975.

Leaman, Oliver. *Introduction to Medieval Islamic Philosophy.* Cambridge, 1985.

Lewis, Bernard. 'Some Observations on the Significance of Heresy in the History of Islam', *Studia Islamica,* 1 (1953), pp.43–63.

——'Politics and War', in J. Schacht and C.E. Bosworth, ed., *The Legacy of Islam,* 2nd. ed., Oxford, 1974, pp.156–209.

Madelung, Wilferd. 'Aspects of Ismāʿīlī Theology: The Prophetic Chain and the God Beyond Being', in S.H. Nasr, ed., *Ismāʿīlī Contributions to Islamic Culture.* Tehran, 1977, pp.51–65.

——'The Sources of Ismāʿīlī Law', *Journal of Near Eastern Studies,* 35 (1976), pp.29–40, reprinted in W. Madelung, *Religious Schools and Sects in Medieval Islam.* London, 1985, article xviii.

——*Religious Trends in Early Islamic Iran.* Albany, NY, 1988.

——*The Succession to Muḥammad: A Study of the Early Caliphate.* Cambridge, 1997.

Mahdi, Muhsin. 'The Rational Tradition in Islam', in F. Daftary, ed., *Intellectual Traditions in Islam.* London, 2000, pp.43–65.

Makdisi, George. 'The Topography of Eleventh Century Baghdad', *Arabica,* 6 (1959), pp.178–97 and pp.281–309.

——'Muslim Institutions of Learning in Eleventh Century Baghdad', *Bulletin of the School of Oriental and African Studies,* 22 (1961), pp.1–56.

——'Ashʿarī and the Ashʿarites in Islamic Religious History', *Studia Islamica,* 17 (1962), pp.37–80 and 18 (1963), pp.19–40.

——'The Marriage of Tughril Beg', *International Journal of Middle East Studies,* 1 (1970), pp.259–75.

——'The Sunnī Revival', in D.S. Richards, ed., *Islamic Civilisation,* pp.155–68.

——*The Rise of Colleges: Institutions of Learning in Islam and the West.* Edinburgh, 1981.

——'Ḥanbalite Islam', in M.L. Swartz, ed. and tr., *Studies on Islam.* New York, 1981, pp.216–74.

——'Authority in the Islamic Community', in G. Makdisi, ed., *La Notion d'autorité au moyen âge: Islam, Byzance, Occident.* Paris, 1982, pp.117–26.

——'The Juridical Theology of Shāfiʿī: Origins and Significance of *Uṣūl al-fiqh*', *Studia Islamica,* 59 (1984), pp.5–48.

——*The Rise of Humanism in Classical Islam and the Christian West: with Special Reference to Scholasticism.* Edinburgh, 1990.

Massignon, Louis. *Recueil de textes inédits concernant l'histoire de la mystique aux pays d'Islam.* Paris, 1929.

al-Māwardī, Abu'l-Ḥasan ʿAlī. *al-Aḥkām al-sulṭaniyya,* ed. R. Enger. Bonn, 1853.

McCarthy, Richard J. *Freedom and Fulfillment.* Boston, 1980.

Mez, Adam. *The Renaissance of Islam*, English tr. S. Khuda Bakhsh and D.S. Margoliouth. New York, 1975.

Mottahedeh, Roy P. 'The Abbasid Caliphate in Iran', in *The Cambridge History of Iran:* Volume 4, *The Period from the Arab Invasion to the Saljuqs*, ed. R.N. Frye. Cambridge, 1975, pp.57–84.

Nanji, Azim. 'Ismā'īlism', in S.H. Nasr, ed., *Islamic Spirituality: Foundations*. London, 1987, pp.179–98.

——'Ismā'īlī Philosophy', in S.H. Nasr and O. Leaman, ed., *History of Islamic Philosophy*. London, 1996, vol.1, pp.144–54.

——'Portraits of Self and Others: Ismaili Perspectives on the History of Religions' in F. Daftary, ed., *Mediaeval Isma'ili History and Thought*. Cambridge, 1996, pp.153–60.

Niẓām al-Mulk. *Siyāsat-nāma*, English tr. Herbert Drake, *The Book of Government or Rules for Kings*. 2nd ed., London, 1978.

Ormsby, Eric. 'The Taste of Truth: The Structure of Experience in al-Ghazālī's *al-Munqidh min al-ḍalāl*', in Wael B. Hallaq and Donald P. Little, ed., *Islamic Studies Presented to Charles J. Adams*. Leiden, 1991, pp.133–52.

——*Theodicy in Islamic Thought: The Dispute over al-Ghazālī's 'Best of all Possible Worlds'*. Princeton, NJ, 1984.

Palacios, Asín. M. *La Espiritualidad de Algazel*. Madrid, 1935.

Poonawala, Ismail K. *Biobibliography of Ismā'īlī Literature*. Malibu, CA, 1977.

Rahman, Fazlur. *Revival and Reform in Islam*, ed. Ebrahim Moosa. Boston, 2000.

Richards, D.S., ed. *Islamic Civilisation, 950–1150*. Oxford, 1973.

Rosenthal, Erwin. *Political Thought in Medieval Islam*. Cambridge, 1962.

Schacht, Joseph. 'Theology and Law in Islam', in G.E. von Grunebaum, ed., *Theology and Law in Islam*, Wiesbaden, 1971, pp.3–23.

——*Introduction to Islamic Law*. Oxford, 1964.

al-Shahrastānī, Muḥammad b. 'Abd al-Karīm. *Kitāb al-Milal wa'l-niḥal*. London, 1846. Partial English tr. A.K. Kazi and J.G. Flynn, *Muslim Sects and Divisions*. London, 1984.

Stern, Samuel M. *Studies in Early Ismā'īlism*. Jerusalem and Leiden, 1983.

Strauss, Leo. *Persecution and the Art of Writing*. Glencoe, IL, 1952.

Tibawi, A.L. 'Al-Ghazālī's Sojourn in Damascus and Jerusalem', *Muslim World*, 9 (1965), pp.198–211.

al-Ṭūṣī, Naṣīr al-Dīn Muḥammad. *Sayr wa sulūk*, ed. and English tr. S.J. Badakhchani, *Contemplation and Action*. London, 1998.
al-Walīd, ʿAlī b. Muḥammad. *Dāmigh al-bāṭil wa ḥatf al-munāḍil*, ed. M. Ghālib. Beirut, 1982.
Walker, Paul E. 'An Ismāʿīlī Answer to the Problem of Worshipping the Unknowable, Neoplatonic God', *American Journal of Arabic Studies*, 2 (1974): pp.7–21.
——*Early Philosophical Shiism: The Ismaili Neoplatonism of Abū Yaʿqūb al-Sijistānī*. Cambridge, 1993.
——*Abū Yaʿqūb al-Sijistānī: Intellectual Missionary*. London, 1996.
——*Hamīd al-Dīn al-Kirmānī: Ismaili Thought in the Age of al-Ḥākim*. London, 1999.
Watt, William Montgomery. 'The Authenticity of the Works Attributed to al-Ghazālī', *Journal of the Royal Asiatic Society* (1952), pp.24–45.
——*Muslim Intellectual: A Study of al-Ghazālī*. Edinburgh, 1963.
——*The Formative Period of Islamic Thought*. Edinburgh, 1973.
——'The Great Community and the Sects', in G.E. Von Grunebaum, ed., *Theology and Law in Islam*. Wiesbaden, 1971, pp.25–36.
—— 'Authority in the Thought of Al-Ghazali', in G. Makdisi, ed., *La Notion d'autorité au moyen âge: Islam, Byzance, Occident*. Paris, 1982, pp.57–67.
Weber, Max. *From Max Weber: Essays in Sociology*, tr. and ed., H.H. Gerth and C.W. Mills. New York, 1959.
Weiss, Bernard G. 'Interpretation in Islamic Law: The Theory of *Ijtihād*', *American Journal of Comparative Law*, 26 (1978), pp.199–212.
——'Knowledge of the Past: The Theory of Tawātur According to Ghazālī', *Studia Islamica*, 61 (1985), pp.81–105.
——'Exotericism and Objectivity in Islamic Jurisprudence', in Nicholas Heer, ed., *Islamic Law and Jurisprudence: Studies in Honour of Farhat J. Ziadeh*. Seattle, 1990, pp.53–72.
——'Law in Islam and in the West: Some Comparative Observations', in Wael B. Hallaq and Donald P. Little, ed., *Islamic Studies Presented to Charles J. Adams*. Leiden, 1991, pp.239–54.
——*The Search for God's Law: Islamic Jurisprudence in the Writings of Sayf al-din Amidi*. Salt Lake City, Utah, 1992.

Index